DEBUNKING NEOLIBERAL DOGMA

SIMPLE RESPONSES TO 20 COMMON ARGUMENTS FOR THE OMNIPOTENCE OF THE NEO-LIBERAL GOD

BY GAVIN N. KAAR

First published April 2021.

ISBN: 9798732321463

DEDICATED TO CYRIL AND IRIS.
JASON QUINN FOR HIS INVALUABLE CONTRIBUTION.
ALSO DEDICATED TO THE SHOULDERS ON WHICH I STAND IN THIS FIELD. MOST NOTABLY MY UNWITTING MENTOR: PETER JOSEPH. NOTHING HAPPENS IN ISOLATION.

PREFACE

This is not meant to be a book of high literature nor a book of in-depth research, the author wishes for the argument against the established socio-economic status quo to be structured in an easily accessible format for the widest reach of people that is possible.

To this end, the book retains a conversational tone focusing on the ease of use against the most common arguments from a layman that has been sufficiently placated by established norms. Established norms, of which the author poses have been institutionalised into society and maintain a general consistency throughout the population.

I have no credentials in socio economics to impress you with but I believe my humble level of knowledge, of which this book is written, is testament to the fact that anyone in society can be part of this conversation and no one is excluded. Anyone can have direct input into the very systems that control us and have a say in our part as a species in the wider ecosystem.

I am, however, highly educated in environmental protection and it's abundantly clear to me that the state of the environment on Earth is wholly dependent on the socio-economic system that the species homo sapiens uses to interact with it. Therefore, my professional role as an environmental protector and avid scholar of socio economics are really one and the same.

Succinctly, there is no single person who makes decisions which purposefully corrupts politicians, that makes people work long hours in unfulfilling jobs, that destroys the environment, that is brutally inhumane to animals, that abuses children and women; rather, people are nodes in a network that work in tandem to produce the socio-economic system we see today.

The throes of this system are largely uncontrollable, and with devastating effect. A general web of acceptance for the 'free-market' God, aggressive defense for its unquestionable status quo power and apathy for any change, combined with the label of infidelity for even discussing change come together to form the neo-liberal dogma we suffer today.

This book therefore wishes, and the author is aware of how ambitious this may seem in relation to how distorted the view on the ability for economic change has become, to tackle this religious acceptance, break down this inherent defensiveness and help galvanise the apathetic masses in the pursuit of making socio-economic changes. Changes based on altruism, cooperation and equality. Changes that *can* achieve homeostasis with our beautiful planet.

TABLE OF CONTENTS

INTRODUCTION

This book intends to provide easily accessible counterarguments to many of the most common arguments for the omnipotence of the neo-liberal god. Peter Joseph, author of *'The New Human Rights Movement'* goes so far as to say this dogma has become so pervasive as to be *"full blown religious extremism"*. Neo liberalism is the god we must bow to and the market is the tool with which he doth command. The current form of the market we call free market capitalism is the modern manifestation of social dominance cloaked in the guise of free trade and democracy, yet the underlying concept of domination remains basically the same since pre-history. This God has become so dominant as to be dogmatic, with any alternative posed quickly struck down and condemned as sacrilegious. The end goal is neoliberal globalisation, homogenising the world into one economic system with the dominant minority at the very top, casting the commandments from on high.

This book humbly hopes to offer support in the conversation to break through this shroud of dogma full of fallacies, rhetoric, jargon and blatant lies. To show that this monotheistic belief system has most of us in trance and the negative effects of this are devastating, deadly and disastrous for us all. It hopes to show that neo liberalism is not omnipotent, that we are not stuck in a monotheistic world of markets and that we can choose our own beliefs, way of life and structure to society.

We can turn the corner and become a true civilization, step away from our primitive barbaric past and step toward a just, civil, structurally organized, supportive and truly equal society where the punishments of not being 'the fittest' does not mean a street, starvation or premature death.

'Fittest' was articulated by Darwin to mean the most able to adapt to the environment. The realisation now must be that we *do* need to adapt to the environment as a species and this now means managing our interaction with the environmental system (the economy) in a frugal thrifty fashion and meeting the limits the environment sets. Basically, achieving homeostasis with the planet. This cannot be achieved within a dogma of the exact opposite of that: through the exploitation of labour and resources: maximise individual monetary profit. Accumulate and grow.

This book assumes the reader understands the failures of this economic mode. The tools offered, to the already neo-liberal god atheist, hope to give a foundation to better articulate the counterargument in response to the Neo-liberal god's omnipotence in an attempt to tackle the shroud with which is presented as 'freedom' and that the neo-liberal god is omnipotent, unique, and unquestionable, holding that shroud over us all. From there, the book hopes to provide a good springboard for further debate into the topic of a more sane socio-economic system in homeostasis with the environment on which it sits.

Finally, an apology must be made at the outset with regard to the quantity of repetition of some of the main points. This is not intentional, but the various arguments have various interlinked comparisons and most are explained by a fundamental flawed belief that sometimes requires repetition to get the full picture. The terms neo-liberalism, the market, capitalism and free market capitalism are used liberally throughout. The main point is the social structure that is used to dominate and control the majority, now achieved under the guise of freedom, its modern name: neo liberalism, the modern mechanism: free market capitalism, the core concept of domination: the same.

However, if you're reading this and are still questioning the nature or source of the problems in the 21st century, the following article will give a historical and succinct perspective of neo liberalism, the ideology that currently keeps this rapacious beast fed, the beast we call 'free market capitalism.'

I humbly wish to insert/quote, arguably, the most coherent, legible and fair judge of this subject: George Monbiot. With an article he wrote in April 2016 for The Guardian, entitled *'Neoliberalism – the ideology at the root of all our problems'*. Arguably his finest article: due to its accessibility and concise illumination of this obscure beast.

The article provides a great summary of the deity; this book itself offers basic tools to help tackle the adherents but for an in-depth understanding of the history, complexities, preconditions and modern manifestations of our current economic mode I suggest *'The New Human Rights Movement'* by Peter Joseph. Joseph's book will be referenced and quoted through out.

NB: the neo-liberal adherents are not only the ones who have been generously rewarded by the system, and will obviously claim 'it works'. But neo-liberalism is so pervasive that it has managed to gain support from its victims too. Strangely; the ones that are most affected by it are the majority. Best described by Joseph, in his book, he succinctly summarises his study of Antonio Gramsci's work on cultural hegemony and the idea of social domination in that, generally speaking, society is conditioned *"to support the worldview of the ruling class. In doing so, they tend to support the mechanisms and institutions that actually oppress them"*. For ease, we will label both the generously rewarded- oblivious-lucky ones and the unwitting victims as Neo-Liberal Victims (NLVs).

The article then, in the vein of not daring to try reinvent this perfectly manufactured wheel:

"Neoliberalism – the ideology at the root of all our problems[1]
Imagine if the people of the Soviet Union had never heard of
communism. The ideology that dominates our lives has, for most of
us, no name. Mention it in conversation and you'll be rewarded
with a shrug. Even if your listeners have heard the term before, they
will struggle to define it. Neoliberalism: do you know what it is?
Its anonymity is both a symptom and cause of its power. It has
played a major role in a remarkable variety of crises: the financial
meltdown of 2007-8, the offshoring of wealth and power, of which
the Panama Papers offer us merely a glimpse, the slow collapse of
public health and education, resurgent child poverty, the epidemic
of loneliness, the collapse of ecosystems, the rise of Donald Trump.
But we respond to these crises as if they emerge in isolation,
apparently unaware that they have all been either catalysed or
exacerbated by the same coherent philosophy; a philosophy that has
– or had – a name. What greater power can there be than to operate
namelessly?

**Inequality is recast as virtuous. The market ensures that everyone
gets what they deserve.**
So pervasive has neoliberalism become that we seldom even
recognise it as an ideology. We appear to accept the proposition that
this utopian, millenarian faith describes a neutral force; a kind of
biological law, like Darwin's theory of evolution. But the
philosophy arose as a conscious attempt to reshape human life and
shift the locus of power.
Neoliberalism sees competition as the defining characteristic of
human relations. It redefines citizens as consumers, whose
democratic choices are best exercised by buying and selling, a
process that rewards merit and punishes inefficiency. It maintains
that "the market" delivers benefits that could never be achieved by
planning.

Attempts to limit competition are treated as inimical to liberty. Tax and regulation should be minimised, public services should be privatised. The organisation of labour and collective bargaining by trade unions are portrayed as market distortions that impede the formation of a natural hierarchy of winners and losers. Inequality is recast as virtuous: a reward for utility and a generator of wealth, which trickles down to enrich everyone. Efforts to create a more equal society are both counterproductive and morally corrosive. The market ensures that everyone gets what they deserve.

We internalise and reproduce its creeds. The rich persuade themselves that they acquired their wealth through merit, ignoring the advantages – such as education, inheritance and class – that may have helped to secure it. The poor begin to blame themselves for their failures, even when they can do little to change their circumstances.

Never mind structural unemployment: if you don't have a job it's because you are unenterprising. Never mind the impossible costs of housing: if your credit card is maxed out, you're feckless and improvident. Never mind that your children no longer have a school playing field: if they get fat, it's your fault. In a world governed by competition, those who fall behind become defined and self-defined as losers. Neoliberalism has brought out the worst in us.

Among the results, as Paul Verhaeghe documents in his book 'What About Me?' are epidemics of self-harm, eating disorders, depression, loneliness, performance anxiety and social phobia. Perhaps it's unsurprising that Britain, in which neoliberal ideology has been most rigorously applied, is the loneliness capital of Europe. We are all neoliberals now.
The term neoliberalism was coined at a meeting in Paris in 1938. Among the delegates were two men who came to define the

ideology, Ludwig von Mises and Friedrich Hayek. Both exiles from
Austria, they saw social democracy, exemplified by Franklin
Roosevelt's New Deal and the gradual development of Britain's
welfare state, as manifestations of a collectivism that occupied the
same spectrum as Nazism and communism.

In The Road to Serfdom, published in 1944, Hayek argued that
government planning, by crushing individualism, would lead
inexorably to totalitarian control. Like Mises's book Bureaucracy,
The Road to Serfdom was widely read. It came to the attention of
some very wealthy people, who saw in the philosophy an
opportunity to free themselves from regulation and tax. When, in
1947, Hayek founded the first organisation that would spread the
doctrine of neoliberalism – the Mont Pelerin Society – it was
supported financially by millionaires and their foundations.

With their help, he began to create what Daniel Stedman Jones
describes in Masters of the Universe as "a kind of neoliberal
international": a transatlantic network of academics, businessmen,
journalists and activists. The movement's rich backers funded a
series of think tanks which would refine and promote the ideology.
Among them were the American Enterprise Institute, the Heritage
Foundation, the Cato Institute, the Institute of Economic Affairs, the
Centre for Policy Studies and the Adam Smith Institute. They also
financed academic positions and departments, particularly at the
universities of Chicago and Virginia.
As it evolved, neoliberalism became more strident. Hayek's view
that governments should regulate competition to prevent
monopolies from forming gave way – among American apostles
such as Milton Friedman – to the belief that monopoly power could
be seen as a reward for efficiency.

Something else happened during this transition: the movement lost its name. In 1951, Friedman was happy to describe himself as a neoliberal. But soon after that, the term began to disappear. Stranger still, even as the ideology became crisper and the movement more coherent, the lost name was not replaced by any common alternative.

At first, despite its lavish funding, neoliberalism remained at the margins. The post-war consensus was almost universal: John Maynard Keynes's economic prescriptions were widely applied, full employment and the relief of poverty were common goals in the US and much of Western Europe, top rates of tax were high and governments sought social outcomes without embarrassment, developing new public services and safety nets.

But in the 1970s, when Keynesian policies began to fall apart and economic crises struck on both sides of the Atlantic, neoliberal ideas began to enter the mainstream. As Friedman remarked, "when the time came that you had to change ... there was an alternative ready there to be picked up". With the help of sympathetic journalists and political advisers, elements of neoliberalism, especially its prescriptions for monetary policy, were adopted by Jimmy Carter's administration in the US and Jim Callaghan's government in Britain.

It may seem strange that a doctrine promising choice should have been promoted with the slogan 'there is no alternative'

After Margaret Thatcher and Ronald Reagan took power, the rest of the package soon followed: massive tax cuts for the rich, the crushing of trade unions, deregulation, privatisation, outsourcing and competition in public services. Through the IMF, the World Bank, the Maastricht treaty and the World Trade Organisation, neoliberal policies were imposed – often without democratic

consent – on much of the world. Most remarkable was its adoption among parties that once belonged to the left: Labour and the Democrats, for example. As Stedman Jones notes, "it is hard to think of another utopia to have been as fully realised."
It may seem strange that a doctrine promising choice and freedom should have been promoted with the slogan "there is no alternative". But, as Hayek remarked on a visit to Pinochet's Chile – one of the first nations in which the programme was comprehensively applied – "my personal preference leans toward a liberal dictatorship rather than toward a democratic government devoid of liberalism". The freedom that neoliberalism offers, which sounds so beguiling when expressed in general terms, turns out to mean freedom for the pike, not for the minnows.

Freedom from trade unions and collective bargaining means the freedom to suppress wages. Freedom from regulation means the freedom to poison rivers, endanger workers, charge iniquitous rates of interest and design exotic financial instruments. Freedom from tax means freedom from the distribution of wealth that lifts people out of poverty.
As Naomi Klein documents in The Shock Doctrine, neoliberal theorists advocated the use of crises to impose unpopular policies while people were distracted: for example, in the aftermath of Pinochet's coup, the Iraq war and Hurricane Katrina, which Friedman described as "an opportunity to radically reform the educational system" in New Orleans.
Where neoliberal policies cannot be imposed domestically, they are imposed internationally, through trade treaties incorporating "investor-state dispute settlement": offshore tribunals in which corporations can press for the removal of social and environmental protections. When parliaments have voted to restrict sales of cigarettes, protect water supplies from mining companies, freeze energy bills or prevent pharmaceutical firms from ripping off the

state, corporations have sued, often successfully. Democracy is reduced to theatre.

Neoliberalism was not conceived as a self-serving racket, but it rapidly became one

Another paradox of neoliberalism is that universal competition relies upon universal quantification and comparison. The result is that workers, job-seekers and public services of every kind are subject to a pettifogging, stifling regime of assessment and monitoring, designed to identify the winners and punish the losers. The doctrine that Von Mises proposed would free us from the bureaucratic nightmare of central planning has instead created one. Neoliberalism was not conceived as a self-serving racket, but it rapidly became one. Economic growth has been markedly slower in the neoliberal era (since 1980 in Britain and the US) than it was in the preceding decades; but not for the very rich. Inequality in the distribution of both income and wealth, after 60 years of decline, rose rapidly in this era, due to the smashing of trade unions, tax reductions, rising rents, privatisation and deregulation.
The privatisation or marketisation of public services such as energy, water, trains, health, education, roads and prisons has enabled corporations to set up tollbooths in front of essential assets and charge rent, either to citizens or to government, for their use. Rent is another term for unearned income. When you pay an inflated price for a train ticket, only part of the fare compensates the operators for the money they spend on fuel, wages, rolling stock and other outlays. The rest reflects the fact that they have you over a barrel.

Those who own and run the UK's privatised or semi-privatised services make stupendous fortunes by investing little and charging much. In Russia and India, oligarchs acquired state assets through firesales. In Mexico, Carlos Slim was granted control of almost all landline and mobile phone services and soon became the world's richest man.

Financialisation, as Andrew Sayer notes in Why We Can't Afford the Rich, has had a similar impact. "Like rent," he argues, "interest is ... unearned income that accrues without any effort". As the poor become poorer and the rich become richer, the rich acquire increasing control over another crucial asset: money. Interest payments, overwhelmingly, are a transfer of money from the poor to the rich. As property prices and the withdrawal of state funding load people with debt (think of the switch from student grants to student loans), the banks and their executives clean up.

Sayer argues that the past four decades have been characterised by a transfer of wealth not only from the poor to the rich, but within the ranks of the wealthy: from those who make their money by producing new goods or services to those who make their money by controlling existing assets and harvesting rent, interest or capital gains. Earned income has been supplanted by unearned income. Neoliberal policies are everywhere beset by market failures. Not only are the banks too big to fail, but so are the corporations now charged with delivering public services. As Tony Judt pointed out in Ill Fares the Land, Hayek forgot that vital national services cannot be allowed to collapse, which means that competition cannot run its course. Business takes the profits, the state keeps the risk.

The greater the failure, the more extreme the ideology becomes. Governments use neoliberal crises as both excuse and opportunity to cut taxes, privatise remaining public services, rip holes in the social safety net, deregulate corporations and re-regulate citizens. The self-hating state now sinks its teeth into every organ of the public sector.

Perhaps the most dangerous impact of neoliberalism is not the economic crises it has caused, but the political crisis. As the domain of the state is reduced, our ability to change the course of our lives through voting also contracts. Instead, neoliberal theory asserts, people can exercise choice through spending. But some have more to spend than others: in the great consumer or shareholder democracy, votes are not equally distributed. The result is a disempowerment of the poor and middle. As parties of the right and former left adopt similar neoliberal policies, disempowerment turns to disenfranchisement. Large numbers of people have been shed from politics.

Chris Hedges remarks that "fascist movements build their base not from the politically active but the politically inactive, the 'losers' who feel, often correctly, they have no voice or role to play in the political establishment". When political debate no longer speaks to us, people become responsive instead to slogans, symbols and sensation. To the admirers of Trump, for example, facts and arguments appear irrelevant.

Judt explained that when the thick mesh of interactions between people and the state has been reduced to nothing but authority and obedience, the only remaining force that binds us is state power. The totalitarianism Hayek feared is more likely to emerge when governments, having lost the moral authority that arises from the delivery of public services, are reduced to "cajoling, threatening and ultimately coercing people to obey them".

Like communism, neoliberalism is the God that failed. But the zombie doctrine staggers on, and one of the reasons is its anonymity. Or rather, a cluster of anonymities.
The invisible doctrine of the invisible hand is promoted by invisible backers. Slowly, very slowly, we have begun to discover the names of a few of them. We find that the Institute of Economic Affairs,

which has argued forcefully in the media against the further regulation of the tobacco industry, has been secretly funded by British American Tobacco since 1963. We discover that Charles and David Koch, two of the richest men in the world, founded the institute that set up the Tea Party movement. We find that Charles Koch, in establishing one of his thinktanks, noted that "in order to avoid undesirable criticism, how the organisation is controlled and directed should not be widely advertised".

The nouveau riche were once disparaged by those who had inherited their money. Today, the relationship has been reversed.

The words used by neoliberalism often conceal more than they elucidate. "The market" sounds like a natural system that might bear upon us equally, like gravity or atmospheric pressure. But it is fraught with power relations. What "the market wants" tends to mean what corporations and their bosses want. "Investment", as Sayer notes, means two quite different things. One is the funding of productive and socially useful activities, the other is the purchase of existing assets to milk them for rent, interest, dividends and capital gains. Using the same word for different activities "camouflages the sources of wealth", leading us to confuse wealth extraction with wealth creation.

A century ago, the nouveau riche were disparaged by those who had inherited their money. Entrepreneurs sought social acceptance by passing themselves off as rentiers. Today, the relationship has been reversed: the rentiers and inheritors style themselves entrepreneurs. They claim to have earned their unearned income.

These anonymities and confusions mesh with the namelessness and placelessness of modern capitalism: the franchise model which ensures that workers do not know for whom they toil; the companies registered through a network of offshore secrecy regimes so complex that even the police cannot discover the beneficial owners; the tax arrangements that bamboozle governments; the financial products no one understands.

The anonymity of neoliberalism is fiercely guarded. Those who are influenced by Hayek, Mises and Friedman tend to reject the term, maintaining – with some justice – that it is used today only pejoratively. But they offer us no substitute. Some describe themselves as classical liberals or libertarians, but these descriptions are both misleading and curiously self-effacing, as they suggest that there is nothing novel about The Road to Serfdom, Bureaucracy or Friedman's classic work, Capitalism and Freedom.

For all that, there is something admirable about the neoliberal project, at least in its early stages. It was a distinctive, innovative philosophy promoted by a coherent network of thinkers and activists with a clear plan of action. It was patient and persistent. The Road to Serfdom became the path to power.

Neoliberalism's triumph also reflects the failure of the left. When laissez-faire economics led to catastrophe in 1929, Keynes devised a comprehensive economic theory to replace it. When Keynesian demand management hit the buffers in the 70s, there was an alternative ready. But when neoliberalism fell apart in 2008 there was ... nothing. This is why the zombie walks. The left and centre have produced no new general framework of economic thought for 80 years.

Every invocation of Lord Keynes is an admission of failure. To propose Keynesian solutions to the crises of the 21st century is to ignore three obvious problems. It is hard to mobilise people around old ideas; the flaws exposed in the 70s have not gone away; and, most importantly, they have nothing to say about our gravest predicament: the environmental crisis. Keynesianism works by stimulating consumer demand to promote economic growth. Consumer demand and economic growth are the motors of environmental destruction.

What the history of both Keynesianism and neoliberalism show is that it's not enough to oppose a broken system. A coherent alternative has to be proposed. For Labour, the Democrats and the wider left, the central task should be to develop an economic Apollo programme, a conscious attempt to design a new system, tailored to the demands of the 21st century.' Article end.

A thrilling tale to say the least, yet with devastating effects. In appendix A a humble attempt to suggest transition steps to a new system, tailored to the 21st century, have been detailed. Taken most notably from the works of Peter Joseph and described in full detail in his book, suggested above.

The objective of creating a new socioeconomic system does not have a goal nor an ideal utopian structure. The way a species interacts with its environment- or 'economic system' as we've labeled it- needs be fully adaptive to whatever is required by the environment on which it sits. This is discussed more in Appendix B. The bottom line, this is not a moral question but a technical one. The environment has a limited carrying capacity- that is to say, our economic system can only consume to this limit, no more. It's that simple- not easy- but simple. From there, a 'genuine' economic system would look to maximize life-supporting resources by maximizing design, production, distribution and recycling techniques within natural limits; with the goal of taming scarcity and ensuring a maximum global health of the population.

With this basic understanding of what a true or genuine economic should be and the true definition of the word 'to economize', we can rightly say neo liberal driven financialised free market capitalism is not economical at all. Therefore, throughout the book we will define this current economic orthodoxy as 'orthodox economics', in terms of the study of the game of markets. We will use 'genuine economics' to define the study of the technical question of economizing our interaction with the environment.

The appendices are a proposition on the attempt to understand the biopsychosocial nature of the human condition and how that understanding can be used in tandem with current technologies to ratchet up socio-activism. How then to galvanise the concerned in a concerted fashion to advance the transition away from barbarism into a true civilization that is in harmony with the environment on which it depends. In a sentence: *Understanding the human condition to attain homeostasis with the planet, coupling the economic system to the environmental system.*

In Chapter 1, we will look at the foundational argument that every NLV reverts back to as soon as common sense and logic thwarts their dogmatic beliefs; '*Humans are greedy*'.

CHAPTER 1:   HUMANS ARE GREEDY

"We are built as gene machines and cultured as meme machines, but we have the power to turn against our creators. We, alone on earth, can rebel against the tyranny of the selfish replicators"

— Richard Dawkins, *The Selfish Gene*

If you haven't read *The Selfish Gene*[2], I highly recommend it. The point made is of most importance and essentially core to this chapter. We are made of selfish genes, selfish in the manner that each gene is only concerned for its own propagation, although it must work with others in a vehicle (our bodies) to try be a gene that propagates.

Within a group of 7.5 billion people on a finite planet, cooperation to control our selfishness is actually the selfish way forward- if you can wrap your head around that mind twister? Essentially, to be in a position to propagate our own genes we need to be able to control how all the genes/individuals are operating together. Because, currently, as a group, if we continue, we'll destroy our genes and everyone else's too, as each individual is working selfishly. It can result in the whole species suffering, as we can now see in the 21st century.

However, as sentient beings, we have the option to control this selfishness as sentient civilised beings and work with regard to the whole species. That is, really, the beauty of how advanced our genes have become; through selfishness, they have propagated to give us the brains to understand that selfishness is no longer the appropriate approach for species propagation: cooperation is now required.

This requires us to remove the 'humans are selfish, greedy and cruel' argument and realise that we are perfectly capable of producing an environment where humans are 'selfless, altruistic and pleasant'. As also presented in Dawkins' book there are studies of cooperation being a triumphant strategy when interacting in a group.

Problematic to this however: the majority of people have no faith in humanity as a whole due to the conditions in which they were reared: a cyclical cognitive flaw. The logical argument is not seen, in that the values they hold and the actions with which they prescribe their judgment are fully encased in a system that encourages and rewards the negative morals and ethics with which they perceive as 'human nature'. As articulated succinctly in the new human rights movement referenced below for further reading on this[3].

This self-imposed posturing, flaunting of wealth and decadence, compounded by the apathetic masses subdued watching cooking/wedding/dancing/singing shows is having deadly effects on us all. The individual's harmless selfishness in tandem with the tide of selfish narcissism is going to destroy everything. Their idiotic narcissistic posturing needs be viewed as what it truly is: a neurological disease.

I believe this must be step one, to appeal to people's noble virtues: to proclaim avidly that humanity can easily be one of caring, altruistic, civilised, cooperative and empathic people. We merely need a system that supports and encourages that part of our nature, henceforth seeing 'good' morals, ethics and positive actions flourish. Controlling the singular selfish gene in the interest of the larger system, in this case the planet and our longevity on it, is the logical next step in the human condition.

An analogy; One does not concern oneself with the method of pruning plants when the soil is polluted/contaminated. Clean the soil first. To have a strategic plan for pruning, watering and caring for plants in the most effective and economic fashion is prudent. However, an understanding that the soil needs to be clean, nutritious and healthy *first* is the most prudent. Otherwise all our efforts to grow healthy, happy and productive plants will be in vain.

Yet, our common perception is one of humanity stuck in a cycle of xenophobic fervour, racist bigotry and prejudicial hatred. So we must try breakdown this shroud that's held over our heads, this religious dogma that's instilled itself in all our heads. This reptilian mental knee-jerk reaction 'humans are greedy and cruel'. How reductive, short sighted and simplistic I find that response.

Below are some arguments commonly presented by NLVs on how humans are inherently flawed, always have been and always will be inherently flawed. A sample simple direct response is given followed by a more detailed critique. Finally, briefly at times, my opinion how this might look in a more advanced economic system that's more in tune with the environment on which it rests.

Understanding a full concept is best achieved by the ability to explain it to yourself in metaphor. Therefore, during conversation with an NLV, we can find ourselves with the ability to bespoke the response, below are just samples I've personally come across. *'Capture their hearts and the mind will follow'*.

1. HUMANS ARE COMPETITIVE, GREEDY AND CRUEL

Sample direct response

Are you the judge on what human nature is?

Is human nature not judged on how people interact with one another? And their environment will have a major influence on that, right? If we've been struggling with crappy farming tools, tough winters and fast animals for thousands of years, is it any wonder human nature is perceived in that way? Wouldn't we have a different idea of human 'nature' if humanity lived in an environment of abundance where no one had to steal from anyone else?

Quick explanation of where the NLV is coming from

This knee-jerk reaction usually comes when the NLV has no further argument and uses it to fall back on. It's essentially the foundation to support the vast inequality and degradation we see today. Usually preceded by the words, 'Well, that will never work because…' or 'That *might* work for a time, but it will revert back to the problems we see today because…'

Isn't it terrible that people need to find a way out of a debate they are losing by using something so despicable as 'humans are cruel' to justify their point and the system they are defending?

Defending might be too strong a word here, they are only defending it due to some form of an evolutionary reptilian knee-jerk reaction, they perceive you are attacking them personally. It's all they've ever known. Change is scary.

But does it not speak volumes of how inherently flawed this system is? That the foundation of it is supported on the 'fact' that humans are cruel and greedy. Essentially, the system only works if humans are accepted as being cruel and greedy. That fact alone should be enough for the NLV to repent on his NL sins.

Basically, with this foundation of 'factual' knowledge, the inequality you see is O.K. and normal. Don't bother trying to change anything. Brutal poverty is a natural thing. It can't be changed so just forget about all the suffering in the world.

This is just preposterous and frankly dogmatic. This philosophical foundationalism (or foundation of 'factual' knowledge) is archaic. A more appropriate method of assessment would be using a tool called epistemological coherentism. Where we have various sources of information and we find justification for each as it coheres to the rest. This is not the place to discuss that but noteworthy and recommended for the avid reader in discussions on the sources of knowledge.

Bottom line:
Is it so hard to fathom a pleasant and altruistic world? And an economic system (our interaction with each other and the environment) based on that? The level of 'greed' we experience in society is a symptom, not a precondition of the system.

An elaboration/critique of the main point/s of the NLV's Argument
An analogy here I find explains the fallacy succinctly:
If you have contaminated soil and all your plants grow to be infected with some disease, is it the fault of the plants? If for 12,000 years we've had the same soil conditions, is it any wonder plants grow to be infected and are assumed to be infectious type plants? If we cleansed the soil would healthy plants not grow?

Since the neo-lithic revolution resources have been sequestered into a controlled environment, places with more resources than others then are envied, hence prone to attack due to the threat of hunger. This has produced fences, tribes, chiefs, boundaries, armies, war, nations and dictators. Before the neo-lithic revolution, it is widely known, man was community-driven and lived in a sharing environment for the most part, and resources were difficult to get but abundant. To quote Robert Sapolsky, neurologist at Stanford: *"Agriculture allowed for the stockpiling of resources and thus, inevitably, the unequal stockpiling of them- stratification of society and the invention of classes. Thus it has allowed for the invention of poverty"* [4].

The 'nature' with which we presume is wholly dependent on the society/environment in which we live or have lived. Humans are adaptable, changing and malleable. Human nature cannot be seen as rigid, isolated or fixed- it's a spectrum. There are only actions and reactions to pre-conditions and manifestations in their environment resulting from interactions within it.

Furthermore, in complete contrast to what contemporary society encourages you to do (i.e. get a Ferrari, millions of dollars, a private jet and consume as much as possible) there are vast swaths of society that completely reject that and pursue a life of frugality, volunteering over 200 billions dollars worth of time to help out in 2019 alone[5]. The broad stroke assumption that 'humans are greedy' does not then apply to them? Further, would the people that are greedy in the current system still be so in a system that did not encourage that behaviour?

We currently have a system, and have done for 12,000 years, based on a fixed level of scarcity. We farmed these scarce resources, put fences up around them and fought each other for them. This competition produced inequality, this inequality produced poverty. This poverty produced behavioural violence. This behavioural violence gives the majority of people the idea that 'all humans are cruel, greedy, competitive'. And, as for the ones fed up and tired of it: lazy.

The current system is structured to encourage the worst parts of our nature, i.e. narcissism, domination, self-maximisation, greed, gluttony etc. to hypothetically have a system that encourages the better parts i.e. altruism, cooperation, selflessness, then we have further seen what human nature can be and can make a more educated guess.

From an epistemological coherent perspective this seems the more apt way to assess what human nature is. Basically, we can only say what it may be when we understand all the other factors that effect it and can infer they are also true be cause of each other, not because some God said so. Bottom line, it's abundantly complex and we may never have a definite answer to what 'human nature' exactly is.

But one thing is clear: it is not what is thrown about today, this 'humans are cruel' presumption is blatant foundationalism and requires that you agree with the 'undeniable fact' cast down from the neo-liberal god that 'humans are greedy and cruel' and no further investigation is required. It is foundational. The only thing we have is a circa 5,000 year recorded history, in a scarce environment during a circa 300,000 year history of homo sapiens and millions of years of animals very similar to us. Were we always cruel and greedy? Studies show we were quite the opposite pre neo lithic revolution[6].

Who knows for certain? Not me! But I do know the argument is inherently flawed, reductive and the person who poses it is most certainly not the judge. Remind them of that.

How might an actual civilised society approach this?
In a more sane socio-economic system- one in which the focus is to
remove poverty, not create it- an abundance of the necessities of life
can be realised. When this is achieved, you immediately remove the
preconditions for the majority of the negative violent behaviour we
see today. You also remove the pre-condition for the negative
behaviour we see around, amongst others such as: theft, fraud,
coercion, sex trafficking. The majority of today's crime and negative
violent behaviour has its precondition in poverty. Remove poverty
and you'll remove the human nature is cruel and greedy attitude.

Essentially, people wouldn't feel the need to fight, steal or be
coercive if they already had a full belly and a warm bed, essentially:
access to resources. With abundant resources; crime would plummet.
People would then say human nature is 'friendly, pleasant and
altruistic'. The pragmatics of having a system that tries to maximise
abundance of resources and provide free access to them is discussed
further in appendix A under 'notes on themes'.

Sample direct response

Fittest in that context, coined by Darwin some 200 years ago, has been bastardised to mean strongest or most dominant. In reality, it means the ability to adapt to the environment. By no stretch of the imagination are we adapting to the environment today. We are adapting the environment to us, but blatantly in a negative fashion that threatens our survival.

Quick explanation of where the NLV is coming from

This reaction usually comes when the NLV needs to justify a point on inequality. Again, it's a foundational point used to support or as a basis for the whole system of inequality and the poverty and negative behaviour resulting. Without the NLV's indoctrinated mind to automatically accept that 'it's survival of the fittest', the vast array of negative manifestations of the market would be most certainly unacceptable. Only when she accepts this fallacy can she accept that some children live in disease and walk over someone as they die in a gutter starved.

This statement is usually preceded by something along the lines of *'that's terrible but…'* or *'There's not enough to go around so it's….'*

This is so offensive and rude that it really smacks of ignorance on the NLV's part. Basically, the suffering is ok because the poor aren't 'strong' enough; in the animal kingdom they kill each other so it's ok for us to do it. Lions eat wildebeest, so we should metaphorically eat the wildebeest too. Mental gymnastics.

Again, does it not speak volumes for the inherent flaws in our current mode of society? Regardless of what label you want to give it, call it, describe it or calculate it, the fact remains: you need to circumnavigate people's innate morals and convince them of something in contradiction to that to be able to gain moral justification for the immoral manifestations of the societal structure.

I.e. Immoral act A is justified because X is constant.
E.g. There is an 11 year life expectancy gap between rich and poor in London...it's survival of the fittest!

Therefore, the societal structure is flawed. Free market capitalism is flawed. And devastatingly so!

X is not constant, here's why, in more detailed an explanation, as I see it.

An elaboration/critique of the main point/s of the NLV's Argument

We are stuck in this loop of justification for blatant over the top negligence, cruelty and downright inhumanity. The UN calculates a poverty line of USD$1.90/day in purchasing power parity (PPP) in 2015 and calculates a total number of just over a billion living in poverty. They use this number in their sustainable development goals and it seems like they have calculated this arbitrary figure just to show that progress has been made on poverty. One can't claim improvement on something just because you moved the goal posts.[7]

The Newcastle University calculated a true or ethical poverty line and details the calculation in full, addressing a range of different caveats and criterion to calculate what it truly requires on a daily basis to meet nutritional needs[8]. When one uses a more appropriate figure to calculate the poverty line, such as $5.50/day we reach a figure of nearly 3.3 billion people, which is about half the population of the world, living in poverty[9]. With this figure, we see that just 8 people have the same wealth as half the population of the world[10]. Can that level of inequality be justified with the argument of 'it's survival of the fittest'? Is there any justification for that level of inequality?

The vast quantity of suffering experienced daily by some 4.5 billion people living below the ethical poverty line, struggling to meet basic nutritional needs, is swept away in a broad sweep with the single statement, 'it's survival of the fittest'. The system is, hence, barbaric.

On a separate side note, the concept is the same so I thought it worth noting. This is also a common argument for continuing to kill and eat meat. Regular arguments with carnivore's result in the comparison of a human being compared with another wild predatory animal. No difference marked between us; one species largely operating on instincts and another with a little box in its pocket that immediately gives it access to information about the intricacies of electrons and neutrons, the nuances of supernovae or what temperature it is currently on the other side of the world. So, the same actions & morals need be applied?

How might an actual civilised society approach this?

Therefore, 'survival of the fittest' in the 21st century actually means a complete re-structure of the socio-economic model because quite simply we are destroying our environment. If we don't adapt our economic system, we will not be fit enough to survive. In a sentence: The economic system is essentially how we interact with the environment as a species, therefore we would need to couple the economic system with the environmental system.

This would require an understanding of the environmental system in its completeness: its full limitations, its resource recuperation rate, an understanding that scarcity is not rigid but fully dependent on how we interact with the resource producing services (an economic system) and a knowledge on how we can best meet those limits. The basis of the economical model needs to be on the resources themselves and how we gather, produce, process, distribute and consume them. This is already been abundantly discussed and lectured; its most advanced label is Natural Law Resource Based Economy (NLRBE). It seems to me a very logical structure to what a new rational economic system would look like, in the true sense of the word. How we get out of the mess we're currently in is the more complicated question. But suggestions on transition are posed in Appendix A.

3. INEQUALITY IS NORMAL, WE ARE ALL GENETICALLY DIFFERENT

Sample direct response

Correct, and diversity is healthy and makes us all better. However, is a system that punishes us- to death sometimes- for being different not barbaric? I mean, the lower rungs of society are treated like animals, living on streets. Even some working class people in supposedly democratic advanced industrial western societies live very abusive, unhealthy and degrading lives. Is it sufficient to say 'we're not equal' as a justification for cruel inhumanity?

Quick explanation of where the NLV is coming from

This argument is usually posed by the NLV as justification for some people working difficult, degrading jobs or the vast array of unequal incomes. It's usually preceded by something along the lines of *'that's terrible but…'* or *'some people have to work those jobs because'* or *'it's ok for him to get that little salary because…'*

The argument is posed as a means to justify in their minds the level of suffering in the world and to placate their helplessness. It's mostly used as a fall-back approach after you've given good examples of brutality directly related to inequality and the NLV has no justification for it. They need to use the fact that 'we're all different' as a means to square in their minds the problems that they are helpless to prevent, mitigate and control. It's a cop-out really, a mental retreat to security, shying away from the problem by using an excuse.

On another note, but relevant, it could otherwise be posed to justify incompetence: *'inequality is normal, I wouldn't want any idiot working on my teeth…'*. This is a whole other argument and best dealt with under the topic of how social mobility is minimal and nobody is born to be a dentist. For example, nothing is in isolation; society is a structure, complex and synergistic. See argument #12, '*Somebody has to do the undesirable work*', for rebuttal and explanation of this fallacy, specifically the last of the leading arguments.

An elaboration/critique of the main point/s of the NLV's Argument

This speaks volumes to the pervasiveness of free market capitalism again. The current socio-economic system has inequality inherent in its make-up and those that are less able or less intelligent to it will be made to serve, suffer and are essentially preyed upon. This tendency of the system to prey upon the 'weak' is appropriately called 'structural violence.' In that, if institutions and structures to society create inequality, then that inequality produces poverty, and that poverty produces violence and then society is structured to be violent.

How blatant a picture can be painted on how flawed a system is, by the view that, regardless of the abundance of people suffering, while some others live in decadent luxury, the level of inequality is unchangeable and perfectly natural. What's worse about this argument is that it's used to justify vast and deep inequality. If we lived in a society where inequality was minimal, then the argument could be held up for debate. But we are talking about inequality on devastating scales here; 8 people with the same wealth as over 3.5 billion people or the fact that there is currently up to a 11 year life expectancy gap between the rich and the poor in London[11].

The NLV is so indoctrinated to this fallacy that the fact that some people are better at using their hands than playing football somehow conflates to footballers deserving to live in 20-room mansions with pools and their own private jets while an unlucky

carpenter ends up living on the street with cardboard and bottles of
1-euro wine.

I can think of no more a bastardisation or mental gymnastics to
allow your mind to make that leap. People are different, I like
football, she likes books, therefore it's ok that she lives on the street.
Mind-boggling! Well, not really mind-boggling when we look at
how well the neo-liberal god has cast down its commandments and
how well they have been accepted by the NLVs. It really *'illustrates
the incredible susceptibility humans have to the demands of the social
system they find themselves in'*, to quote Joseph again.

How might an actual civilised society approach this?

A structure to society where the most able feel proud to be
supporting the least able seems most prudent; it was a lucky draw
after all. A system that frowns upon an able-bodied/minded person
that doesn't pull her weight should be the norm in contrast to a
system that frowns upon a dis-abled/minded person that can't keep
up with the 'able' people.

A modern day example: a 27-year-old fit and healthy man, born to
inheritance with the best of health and education available spends
his time flying and sailing around the world partying, taking
cocaine and lying on beaches while a working-class woman of 60
needs to work 2 jobs while helping with grandkids. Poor health and
education accessibility through her life has kept her there. His
decadence, luxury and leisure is in direct correlation to her
degradation, poverty and difficulties. We must realize this, as a
species. He should feel ashamed for that, not be looked upon with
reverence.

This thought process is articulated perfectly by Joseph: "*a polite level of disrespect and shame should be put upon those promoting high wealth, consumerism and materialism. No longer should any respect or praise be placed on those engaging in conspicuous consumption or wealth signaling. Those driving Ferraris down the street or sporting designer handbags should be made feel embarrassed for their wasteful and insulting decadence. It needs to be communicated that such values only symbolize the structural violence of the world, not the individuals own ostensible success or status. Extreme luxury goods today really signify dehumanization and a lack of empathy*"

But the key point here, and, arguably, the most pertinent in striving for a better system, is that a system structured in this fashion will, quite obviously and naturally, gradually increase the average intelligence and gradually decrease the quantity of 'disabled' people as society will strive to support the least abled, hence alleviating the stress and lifting the standard gradually. We must turn the corner and realise that a civilised society should strive to care for the 'least' of us, recognising that the 'least' of us when cared for will make us all better. Is it not obvious that when your neighbours, colleagues and community are happy, healthy and well educated that you then in turn will be happier too?

Personal opinion

Therefore, the question remains: are you happy to live in a system that is blatantly barbaric and predatory to some people, simply for being born in such a state or situation? Simple analogy: the big bully on the playground who would pick on the weakest of the kids. This is effectively what the current system does, preys on the weak, makes them suffer, coerces them into submission and spits them out.

Essentially, I'd prefer to live in relative poverty in pure equality with my dignity and integrity intact. Would you? The book *the spirit level* by Professors Richard Wilkinson & Kate Pickett give empirical evidence of the negative effects of inequality in great detail[12]. Showing that the more equal society is, the more healthy, happy and productive people are.

Note: Relative poverty is not even required, it has been proven countless times by different studies that we can all live healthy lives with basic necessities met, within the current system if the wealth was spread out more equally[13]. But again, this is basically asking the neo-liberal god to change his spots.

If we had a true economic system, which is discussed in depth in *The New Human Rights Movement*, a very high standard of living could be reached for all.

4. PEOPLE ARE POOR BECAUSE THEY ARE LAZY AND FICKLE

Sample direct response

People are 'lazy' because they're tired from the stress of debt, an 8-hour work day and the lack of satisfaction in work.
And they only seem 'fickle' because they haven't got enough disposable income, as they are living from pay cheque to pay cheque.

Quick explanation of where the NLV is coming from
This argument is usually posed by the NLV as justification for brutal exploitation. Humans need to feel they have worth and are respected. If that is removed, they will lose agency and will appear 'lazy' but really they're just depressed and disillusioned. Basically, if we didn't force them to work, they would laze around on their couches and do nothing. A coercive exploitative system is required.

A socio economic system that requires worker drones puts a certain proportion of people in demeaning labour roles that are undesirable as a natural function of maintaining the hierarchy and inequality status quo.

Specifically, this argument poses that some people are required to work difficult jobs because they are too lazy to get a 'good' job or too lazy to educate themselves properly. It basically states, pretentiously; *'We can all be rich if we work hard'*. Never mind the drastically more advantageous starts in life some people will have in contrast to others, notably the level of accessibility to education and health services. Nor the fact, that it's mathematically impossible for everyone to be rich. The NLV posing the argument would really have to be one of 2 things: 1, complicit in the system of labour

coercion and be happy with the level of inequality or 2, completely
ignorant of how the system works at a fundamental level.

'People are lazy' is usually preceded by statements like: *'That is a
terrible job to have to do but if they would just educate themselves they can
get a better job. The problem is….'* Or *'we need hierarchical systems
otherwise those lazy so & so's wouldn't get off their lazy asses…'*

**An elaboration/critique of the main point/s of the NLVs
Argument**
Obviously the nature of human gumption and/or laziness is an
abundantly complex topic, notwithstanding there are 7.3 billion
people, and again taking a systemic or synergistic perspective of the
problem is the most apt manner with which to address the study of
it. But one thing is certain, you cannot simply say 'people are lazy'
because you see people watching a high quantity of TV in the
evenings instead of being more productive in fixing their problems.

It seems obvious to me that a vicious cycle exists between the stress
of working a full-time job, the need for the market to have worker
drones to exploit and the societal structure that places people into
individualistic units rather than supportive communities. The
system says 'don't be so lazy, go to college and get a professional
job, you can make it- if you work hard' while at the same time,
mathematically, it is not possible for everyone to achieve that.

Furthermore, it is a function of the level of inequality experienced
on a national and international level. We see a 11-year life
expectancy gap between the rich and the poor in London and
similar differences between the rich and wealthy nations. The rich's
decadence is in direct correlation to the poor's degradation.
To then make that mental leap and state the reason they are poor is
due to laziness completely negates the nature of the inequality

machine and its ramifications. Ramifications, which I have stated, are devastating and are submitted on the populous on a structural level and violently so.

It essentially supports the necessity for labour coercion and justifies the hierarchical roles inherent in the system, compounded by a system of institutional control that severely limits the possibility of moving up the social ladder: the mathematical impossibility for everyone to be rich and/or middle class is inherent. The vertigo of late modernity where everyone lives in fear of those below them on the socio-economic ladder, resulting in the nullification of interclass solidarity and justification for the erosion of social safety nets.

It essentially requires an exceptional level of ignorance, stupidity and tunnel vision to conclude 'humans are lazy' from vast levels of inequality, coercion and exploitation. A complete disregard for societies' structure and a blindfolded assumption that everyone can rise to middle class in a system that encourages inequality and requires a worker drone class to function as servants to allow the middle/upper classes to thrive in a lifestyle of luxury.

Again, it speaks volumes on how perverse the system is, that it's required to mould into the minds of the masses that we are lazy. How perverted a system, required to coerce the worker drones into subordination and servitude. It's a system of control and an underlying assumption that everyone can be rich if they weren't so lazy is required, what a lack of dignity and integrity our current socio-economic system has.

A further discussion on how the rich are 'job creators' will be had in the next chapter in argument #5 and a discussion on the conflation of jobs and vocations in life will be had in chapter 5, argument #19.

CHAPTER CONCLUSION

In the interest of naming and shaming current people, organisations or NGOs that are involved in the tackling of these symptoms, it seems apparent to me that this encompasses everyone and every organisation involved in ending oppression in its myriad forms. Anyone involved in, amongst others, environmental degradation mitigation, humanity relief and endangered species protection are all fighting symptoms of a broken economic system based around the *'fact'* that humans are cruel, competitive, self-interested and greedy. Focus your resources instead on the root cause of the problem, which is the game theory of markets that encourages, supports and rewards this behaviour. The contemporary manifestation of this fight for life/earn-a-living zeitgeist has a root orientation in market ideology, namely competition over scarce resources. A concerted effort to tackle the core problem and end oppression seems to me the pertinent route to alleviate the negative outputs we suffer. In Appendix A, a sample idea is conjured.

An incentive system based on cooperation and limited to factors of humanity seems a prudent turn. Possibly community level organisation of 150 people becoming as close to self-sufficient as possible? Huge strides on reducing the working day and or workweek are being made also. This is completely outside the functions of neo liberal free market capitalism and truly achieving a situation of allowing every individual to achieve their full potential and seek a life of agency would first require the removal of poverty completely.

A good example of people regaining their agency and finding purpose in life again with the introduction experimentally of the

Universal Basic Income (UBI) to 16 labour trial programs. The results were fairly exceptional and on average people began to pursue lives and interests within their own accord[14]. With this basic support it's hard to see human nature perccived as greedy and cruel and easier to see behaviour like that as violent outgrowths of an incentive system structured that way.

In the next chapter, a discussion on the arguments based around economics will be attempted. This might get a bit more technical than this chapter but every effort has been made to make it as accessible as possible, maintaining a conversational tone. Can capitalism really solve the poverty problem? Does it not produce brutal inequality on a national and international scale? Isn't that a precursor/precondition for global poverty? Are markets the only we way we can maintain global economics and distribute resources?

CHAPTER 2: IT'S SIMPLE SUPPLY AND DEMAND

"Where there is no free market, there is no pricing mechanism: without a pricing mechanism, there is no economic calculation."
- Ludwig Von Mises, 1922

"It is now highly feasible to take care of everybody on Earth at a higher standard of living than any have ever known. It no longer has to be you or me. Selfishness is unnecessary. War is obsolete. It is a matter of converting the high technology from weaponry to livingry."
- R. Buckminster Fuller, 1981

"One great efficiency flaw in market economics is that it is void of any larger-order design"
- Peter Joseph, 2017

In 1922 Mises wrote that, nearly 100 years ago, yet still the current mode of economics is largely based on that theory, would Mises conclude the same in 2021 with the advent of computation and the ease at which economic calculations could be done now? Correction; *are* being done now: large-scale retail supply chain software exemplary.

What Bucky said 40 years ago was blatantly true. Now, it's just abundantly easier, with an even higher standard of living. The age-old calculation argument is now moot. I think we can all agree that a socio-economic system is basically the organising structure in which we, as a species, interact with the environment. If the organising structure is having negative effects, through incessant consumption[15] on the environment with which it depends, then it is obviously redundant.

All previous socio-economic systems were inherently flawed in this manner; free-market capitalism is no different. It's merely the modern day manifestation of the same old record played over and over again. No thought is given into its core structure, no regard for its externalities, no prudence in being pro-active in the long run, just *'the market will regulate itself'*. This was fine before, when the ramifications were negligible. Now, however, the outcomes are having devastating and deadly global scale negative effects to everyone and everything[16].

Its progression from basic barbarism: 'There's not enough to go around, fight for it, whoever's weak will die, the strong will survive!' to the modern day institutionalised barbarism, where poverty is seen as a natural phenomena. Violence, gangs and war are seen as a natural outcome. Women selling their bodies to survive perceived as normal. A 30-stone person while a child is dying of malnutrition is seen as the 'nature of things'. In the same place, a disease epidemic breaks out that is fully preventable, only a short plane ride away- again, a natural outcome apparently.

To quote professor of sociology Jason Quinn on the historical continuance of barbaric socioeconomic control *'For Marx (1887) the transition from feudalism to capitalism involved distorting the fact that it was a continuation of the subservient relationship between the lord and his serfs albeit with a pluralistic combination of masters playing the role of the feudal lord. To achieve this goal required a fundamental reorientation of the social relations that dictated the life course of the citizen. This necessitated the extraction of the human to be replaced by the object, therefore successfully achieving the dehumanisation of social relations in that they no longer revolved around the relations between individuals rather they were now seen as the social relations between things. This divorced the worker/human from the fruits of their labour and allowed for the commodification of previously uncommodified abstracts such as land, labour and money (Polanyi, 1944)'.*

We are indoctrinated to support a structure of barbarism and neglect.

If a socio-economic system is structured in a certain fashion and results in violence, then *it is* structurally violent. We have structured a system that is violent to itself, its supporting system and its components. Other than the given 'barbaric' and 'negligent' terms of description, apt adjectives of description might be backward, idiotic, redundant, outdated or obsolete.

One could probably turn a blind eye to the silly games that are played all over the world- games like betting on the movement of candlesticks on a screen and moving digits from one screen to a different screen that's on a particular island with particular tax laws- if the results weren't so devastating and deadly. These games, amongst others, are now causing global catastrophe and are further compounded by the decadent flaunts of wealth. This unequal wealth concentration is at the core of global epidemiological problems[17].

Bottom line: limits to the environment exist, whether the neo-liberal god likes it or not. Therefore, we need to couple the economic system to those limits, it's that simple. A saner economic system, therefore, whatever that may look like should have at its core principles of integrity, dignity, respect for one another and the environmental system on which it depends. Again, coupling the economic system to the environmental system is the key. I don't presume to know how a more advanced system might operate in totality but simple core points are obvious: quantify the resources, don't exceed consumption of that quantity (or the replenishment rate) and proclaim them as common heritage to all of humanity. These are components of a genuine economic system, where large order design is inherent; markets just can't cope with global requirements of a planet needing to remain sustainable. This is the focus of this chapter.

Succinctly; the level of disregard for the outputs of their games is now at a level of deadly effect. Concerned and intelligent beings with an understanding of the need to control the individual selfish gene must now act. The first step is to understand this market-related tunnel vision we face and subdue its heaves, blowing back the shroud that is held over the masses to instill an understanding of genuine economics to ensure the removal of poverty and live in sustainability with the planet.

Below, I humbly wish to assist in this endeavour. Here are some arguments regularly posed on how the free market God alone has the power to look after us lowly mortals, we could never have the smarty-smarts to work things out for ourselves and we shouldn't even try.

Again, a sample simple direct response is given, followed by a slightly more detailed critique of the problem and how this problem might be solved or might look in a saner genuine economic system. Understanding a full concept is best achieved by the ability to explain it to yourself in metaphor. Therefore, during conversation with an NLV, we can find ourselves with the ability to bespoke the response, below are just samples I've personally come across. *'Capture their hearts and the mind will follow'*.

Sample direct response

Most jobs are degrading, poorly paid and back-breaking. People need security, food, health, community and meaningful work; please don't confuse that with 'jobs'! Trickledown economics doesn't work and never has, socialism for the rich is inherently corrupt, and reinforces the cycle of exploitation.

What you're really saying here is: yes, there is vast inequality and poverty inherent in the system, but rich people give a small amount of alleviation to a small number of people so aren't they great?

Quick explanation of where the NLV is coming from

The NLV has a fundamental belief here that rich people are required for humanity to progress. This is an attempt by the NLV to revert problems in macro-economics to a micro-economic perspective. It's a distraction tactic argument. They'll usually take this stance after you've highlighted some flaws in the current economic system or if they need to highlight a minor positive. It's usually preceded by something like: *'yes that level of inequality is bad but what are you going to do? Tax the rich some more? We need the rich, they're job creators.'*

On a side but important note here; immediately after this, the NLV will probably state; *'If you raise the tax too high, the rich will just take their business to Monaco'*. A sample response for this has been posed in argument #8 instead as an effort to maintain congruence and structure.

So back to the point: 'jobs'. If we take an example of Twitter perhaps, then yes, the statement can be correct, that jobs have been created, if we frame it in that fashion but don't take a broader systemic perspective and only focus on that tiny fraction of people that otherwise wouldn't have a job. There are macro problems and the NLV suggests a micro alleviation as justification.

As a simplistic example, in the context of Twitter: did high-skilled people currently working in Twitter not have jobs prior, or job potential, before Twitter opened? Is Twitter then a jobs creator or a jobs hole filler? The system requires worker drones so they then have money to consume the products of capitalism. Capitalism requires an unemployment-equilibrium to maintain leverage over people, so they can be more easily pitted against each other, coerced into labour and exploited to the max; hence max profit.
There are macro problems and the NLV suggests a micro alleviation as justification.

Anyway, the real point that the NLV is *trying* to make here is that....'*competition drives our species to progress into new avenues of innovation, hence creating 'jobs' on the way'*. The NLV can rarely articulate that because the majority of them just toe the line of the established arguments. '*Rich people are job creators*' is what they hear over and over again. Take a moment to dismantle their presumptions on what a 'job' means in contemporary neo-liberal capitalism as above and then address the real point they are trying to make:
'Jobs (human progress) are created through competitive innovation'.
The problem with that is that currently most jobs are actually also taken away through innovation as we see with the advent of technological unemployment. This inherent flaw in free market capitalism will be discussed in argument #6 however.

An elaboration/critique of the main point/s of the NLVs Argument

The core flaw of the NLVs' argument here is that human progress or worth is somehow conflated to mean 'Jobs'. When did your job become a metric for judging the worth of a person? Here, we have an abstract point on competitive innovation and a fundamental belief that this is the only way to inspire our species to excel. Second, we have a function of our current economic mode that coerces people into labour positions for money: 'jobs'. This contract for money is essentially debt peonage as we rent our bodies and minds out to capitalist institutions for alleviation of the debt and/or access to resources.

'Jobs', then, are social constructs to coerce one's labour, with the threat of poverty looming overhead; the compulsion to work and the money received; the contract with which you submit.
So, the argument that competitive innovation creates social constructs of coercion and that you should be happy you have them- because, if not, you'll live in poverty- is inherently offensive. Furthermore, you better be grateful or somebody else will take the 'job'. Desperation is used to coerce people into inhumane labour roles to create profit through the medium of 'jobs'. For example the recent rise in the precarious class of jobs. Where zero hour precarious employment is beneficial to the employer, this is ultimately bad for society as it increases feelings of abandonment and disaffection, which will obviously eventually result in social unrest and the rise of right wing populist parties promising the sun, moon and stars that will never come to pass, as we've seen countless times.

Only in a system of brutal control that encourages and rewards dominance can we conclude that creating 'jobs', in that context, is, first, a good thing and, second, justification for the system that produces the very poverty that you are threatened with in the first place.

Competition may well be a driver for innovation but to make the leap and conflate the two points described above is dangerous and as I've alluded to, downright offensive. The potential for competitive innovation to somewhat alleviate brutal inequality, poverty and violence does not give justification for an overarching system that creates that in the first place. Remind them of that.

This is really a fundamental belief that this is the ONLY way to inspire our species to excel. This is the main point here that needs a bit more of a discussion. Because it's actually one where we can apply some critical thinking and where there actually is some form of a debate to be had with these indoctrinated non-critical thinking NLVs.

Firstly, I think it's correct to say competitive innovation is *A* driver for the progression of our species. To posit otherwise is simply incorrect due to our evolution as mammals. But, to jump to the conclusion that a rich person creating 'jobs' in the 21st century is the sole reason for this progression is a huge conflation. Geoff Bezos, the richest man in the world at the moment, didn't come out of the womb with Amazon plans: his progress and the creation of Amazon is a product of society, not solely his individual intellect.

Competitive innovation is definitely *a* driver for this but not the *ONLY* reason why Amazon was created. It's an amalgamation of all of human historical technological advancements, for an NLV to say Geoff Bezos alone is the reason Amazon is here and he alone is the reason a small amount of people will be alleviated temporarily from the threat of poverty is such a reductive and offensive argument. We must be sure to analyse this in full and not allow ourselves to jump to conclusions and conflations.

So in summary, when we unpack the argument, we find we have two parts to the NLVs' argument:

1. Through competitive innovation some people become very rich and create 'jobs' for everyone.
2. Applying competitive innovation will alleviate the negative outcomes that are experienced by our current economic system.

Both ridiculous arguments: the first fallacy I hope I've succinctly discussed above but a further discussion on these two fallacies has been explored in arguments #6 & #7 below. Finally, important to note, in argument #6 we also briefly explore how the public sector has been the real driver of innovation historically, not the private sector.

As an aside, a usual rebuttal to this by the NLV will be *humans like to work*. Humans like to have agency or a vocation. A brief transpose in terminology highlights this. 'Jobs' in the context of coercion and having a vocation in life are two very different things. This is explored more in argument #19.

6. COMPETITIVE INNOVATION WILL EVENTUALLY FIX CAPITALISMS FLAWS

Sample direct response

On the contrary, capitalism will eventually destroy itself through competitive innovation; it's called technological unemployment. Capitalism always looks to improve the bottom line, if that means a robot instead of human then so be it. No workers, no wages, no consumption, no market.

Quick explanation of where the NLV is coming from

This argument is usually posed by the NLV when they have suffered some defeats in the arguments against contemporary market capitalism. Otherwise, it's posed by the NLV when she has some basic understanding on the structures at play and can see holes in the system, but is unwilling to throw the baby out with the bathwater, as the saying goes. The NLV concedes flaws in the system but uses the argument to justify the devastating effects of these flaws and that they are only temporary. Further, that competition is the *only* way to solve the problems.

The argument suggests the system is just maturing and its core functioning will eventually solve the temporary flaws with time. Technology is advancing and, if we allow it to mature, it will eventually fix the flaws and do it quicker than new ones arise. The people that put forth this reasoning have been aptly dubbed techno-capitalist apologists or techno-optimists; Or accelerationists, accelerationism is the belief that ramping up technological innovation will eventually result in a phase of transcendence where capitalism is left behind and a technological utopia will emerge that lifts the entire population of the world up. The flaws in this will be discussed further in argument #7 however.

We never get an idea of how long this will take from them nor do we get a definitive answer on whether the 'exceptional innovation' component can solve new problems quicker than they arise. The beauty of this 'revert back to' argument is that it can be used to justify any flaw, especially when you can finally make them understand that a particular problem we are experiencing as a species is directly related to the core functioning of the current economic mode. In the end, they can always revert back to: '*Yeah, 40,000 people sleeping rough in London tonight is shitty but competitive innovation will eventually fix Capitalism's flaws*'…'*I know it's shitty that 3.4 billion are living in poverty but it's the best system we've got, competitive innovation will eventually fix Capitalism's flaws*'

Bottom line in my opinion, even *1* person sleeping rough or living in poverty is too many. The question is not *should* we change the system; it is just *how?* Using the very system that produces the problem in the first place is most certainly not the solution. Remind them of that.

An elaboration & critique of the main point/s of the NLV's Argument

Again, we need to unpack what the NLV's arguments truly are here.
Underneath the NLV's tow-the-line argument we find two fallacies and find sample responses:

1. No; competitive innovation doesn't fix capitalism's flaws- in fact, it's a major driver for an inherent flaw, called technological unemployment. Using tools in the very system that produces the problem is most certainly not the solution.

2. Technological advancement is actually what drives
    our species forward but this is not due to
    competition, but in spite of it. (This second argument
    will be explored further in argument #7).

So, to further elaborate on the first point:

We must understand that competitive innovation is the crux of the issue behind technological unemployment, without the competitive nature of the system we can't account for blatant indifference in outsourcing labour requirements (jobs) to robots.

If capitalism requires consumers to consume the produce, but at the same time doesn't have 'jobs' to give them money to purchase the produce, we arrive at a core system flaw. Create products- give salary- purchase products- consume products- repeat.

If you remove any of those steps, in the case of robots getting salary (i.e.: robot owners' profits) instead of the public then the system no longer functions. Competitive innovation can rightly be described as the driver for the system to fail, not to succeed. It can rightly be described as the main reason for the core flaw, not some way to fix the over-all flawed system.

We do see some slight alleviation from this as job roles are created in place of others, but this is not the intention, merely a ramification. For example, with the advent of The Green Revolution and the drastic drop in labour in agricultural roles through advanced technological application in farming techniques, the jobs moved into the service sector[18]. Increasing efficiency through technological application made a sector unemployed, so they went into making coffees instead. Where will they go next?

Now we see the service sector being automated more and more and will continue to increase, where will the unemployed go next? Into the precarious sector? Does Uber Eats really need that many scooter drivers? The very definition of this new sector shines a light on the core problem of competition and its drive to automate while forcing people to accept unsecure labour contracts and take whatever they can find to pay the bills. *'Precarity (also precariousness) is a precarious existence, lacking in predictability, job security, material or psychological welfare'. The social class defined by this condition has been termed the precariat* as defined in Wikipedia.

The anthropologist David Graeber wrote a book called *'Bullshit Jobs'* and amusingly wrote *'It's as if someone were out there making up pointless jobs just for the sake of keeping us all working'*. The book is detailed and the reasons are nuanced for the abundance of pointless jobs but I feel on a macro level the argument can be made that it's an overarching need for capitalism to fill 'job' roles to keep the cyclical consumption needs ever flowing. For a full understanding of this phenomenon in contemporary capitalism, I recommend reading the book.

Finally, to confirm the fallacy:
It's now understood it's actually been the public sector that has been at the forefront of financing historical innovation, not the private. Major innovative and technological advancements have been mostly government funded to date[19]. Neo-liberalism actually hinders progress; corporations are only interested in individual short-term profits. Risky long-term ventures hold minimal value on average to the functions of the modern capitalist game. It's only through the public sectors ability to see long term benefits and secure funds for more ambitious endeavours outside the cut-throat game of commerce can we see theoretical ambitious innovative achievements.

Furthermore, to add insult to injury, as a function of the game of international commerce, this technological innovation is used by the wealthy in the world as they see fit and what minor amount 'trickles down' to the poverty stricken areas is not the intention, merely a side effect, nor is what the poverty affected people's need. A pertinent example; in some areas of poverty-stricken Africa, the people have mobile phones but no clean running water, as described by a study done across 35 African countries.[20]

Half the world suffers in poverty and it's growing, as discussed in argument 2. Poverty is an inherent flaw in contemporary capitalism, neo liberalism hopes to solve it with the very mechanisms that produce it. This commandment from the neo-liberal god has to be subverted.

How might a true civilisation perceive this?
The goal of any economic system should be the intention to remove the problems we are experiencing as a society, poverty and climate change the most pertinent in the 21st century.

The application of technology to alleviate arduous labour should be the goal. Automation increases productivity exponentially and would be applied to the most monotonous arduous labour roles first. A true economic system, in the truest sense of that word, would maximise the application of technology on all levels to automate labour.

To quote Joseph: *'rather than enduring the relatively slow process of cost-efficiency-automation, where companies only automate when it is cheaper than human labour, the intent should be full automation overall, favouring full automation'*. Then we would be free to pursue our vocations and have true agency.

7. CAPITALISM HAS LIFTED MILLIONS OF PEOPLE FROM POVERTY

Sample direct response

Was that due to 'capitalism' or due to technological advancements? Or to human ingenuity innovation and compassion? Capitalism forces people into poverty in the first place, by its 'inequality is normal' nature, if anyone got out of poverty it was in spite of it, not because of it. Necessity is the mother of invention…not profit.

Quick explanation of where the NLV is coming from

As we've discussed previously, fundamentally the system produces the flaws of inequality, poverty etc. as a core function. Assuming a failing system will somehow override it's core function in a positive fashion with it's own components is naïve, to say the least.

The point of the NLV's argument is that people globally are seeing an increase in standard of living. Firstly, this increase is extremely moderate and in no way fair for the levels of wealth, resources and calories of food that are actually being produced. It's now a fact that the world produces 2700 calories a day, enough for global hunger to be removed completely but again, the neo liberal God's commandments don't allow for even distribution[21]. Second, The increase is due to technological development and not any supreme function of capitalism or the generosity of the neo-liberal god, as discussed in the previous argument.

A perfect example of the fallacy in this argument is the fact that, according to a 2014 UN report, Africa loses more than it receives financially due to illicit financial flows[22]. This loss or siphoning of the continents wealth directly relates to the poverty experienced by those poor people. The claim that capitalism is saving more people that it is harming is a blatant and deadly lie. It's true people do get lifted from poverty but the reasons for this are nuanced and complicated, mostly due to technology and humanitarian assistance in spite of neo liberalistic free market capitalism.

I could bombard you with figures, studies and graphs showing the wealth disparity globally and the concentration of wealth but this has been done exceptionally well already in the ground breaking, well written and data rich book by Thomas Picketty in 2016, *'Capitalism in the 21st century'* which shows this in great detail. The fact of the matter is this: there is no mechanism inherent in the free market to remove poverty, indeed it is quite the opposite, the inherent logic of the free market is one of exploitation of labour for profit. Removing people from poverty would be antithetical to the very nature of the system. The neo-liberal gods commandments don't allow it. Under neo-liberalism inequality is a necessary part of the system.

Every large institution has basically been set up and now functions on this premise. However well meaning the institutions were at inception or in fact however well meaning the people working within these institutions are now, the neo-liberal god logic will always regress back to the core principal of exploitation for personal profit, regardless of human or environmental concerns. The statement therefore, 'capitalism has lifted people from poverty' is short sighted, truncated and redundant. It is a simple cognitive fallacy, using the term you wish in isolation to justify something that can't be understood without the synergies of the whole system, history and the bio-psychosocial nature of humanity.

Furthermore, to throw salt on the wound, the UN gives an extremely low level of poverty as described in argument #2. If a true level of poverty were given, one that shows peoples basic needs met, then we would have an increase in overall poverty and an increasing rate[23] as calculated by the economic department at the University of Newcastle in the UK. So the argument we are removing overall poverty is largely mute.

Bottom line, the trickle down effect doesn't exist on a sufficient enough scale, if at all. Productivity and wage growth have been decoupled since the 80's, wages have been stagnant[24]. The fact remains; it's a regression, a race to the bottom. Remind them of that.

An elaboration/critique of the main point/s of the NLVs Argument

The main point to discuss here is that there has been an ever-increasing standard of living globally, this is not up for debate, what is up for debate though is the assumption by the NLV that it is all because capitalism is so great and the neo liberal Gods trickle down wand is magical. Essentially, to make the mental gymnastics and conflate capitalism with increased standard of living is a tad presumptuous. I would go so far as to say; it has been in spite of free market capitalism not because of it.

Currently people *are* seeing a better standard of living in places like China, India and Brazil through myriad various geo-political changes, the scope of this book will not be to go into that but suffice to say it is not due to 'capitalism'. One thing we can say with complete confidence however: increased standards of living globally, since the dawn of humanity, has been through technological advancements and the ability of doing more with less. The term coined by R. Buckminster Fuller is ephemeralisation or the modern term used by economists for this phenomenon is zero marginal cost[25]. Most notably Jeremy Rifkin in his book '*the zero marginal cost society: The Internet of Things, the*

Collaborative Commons and the Eclipse of Capitalism'. This basically means that we produce more goods and services, through the application of technology, to maximise efficiency and productivity at an ever-decreasing cost, compounded by the application of the Internet of things (IOT).

Joseph articulates this well over a few pages in his book, which I'll try summarise:

The assumption however is that the '*market is creating the power of increased efficiency when the real cause is our increasing capacity to intelligently design'*.

The major flaw in its reasoning is the idea that '*the market will arrive at a global, zero marginal cost post scarcity condition in environmental harmony all by itself'* and '*we need only tweak the market to birth an abundant, equitable society'*. This perspective does not recognise '*the market is merely an incentive and distribution system, and a poor one at that'*.

It seems to completely overlook the root socioeconomic orientation of the market where competition, exploitation and domination for individual monetary profit is the driver and priority. Slight alleviations via zero marginal cost are secondary. For example: '*a company that sells a good for $5 that costs $3 to make, finding that it can reduce its production cost to $2, does not lower its original selling price if can avoid doing so. The whole point is to increase profits, not equalise them based on production savings'*, this creates self limiting thresholds toward zero marginal cost'

A genuine economic system would be the exact opposite of that, it's goal would be to equalise them until it is actually at zero cost, therefore creating an abundance. Individual monetary profit is irrelevant and not in the equation.

Peter Joseph has coined a term for this point of view in his book *'the new human rights movement'* which I agree is an apt single term description: *"I use the term techno-capitalist apologists to refer to those who view the market as a facilitator of, rather than a hindrance to, material and social progress"*

The problem is this global market game is resulting in major species level problems with vast quantities of people wanting to increase their standard of living, and rightly so, trying to reach the wests level of development. However the west is only developed due to the burning of fossil fuels and the subjugation of the colonised countries through historical imperialism (The luxuries of the west through imperialism will be discussed more in argument #14). In a practical limits sense; if the Global South meets the Wests level of development we would need 27 earths to sustain them in the current mode of economics. This will be discussed in more detail in the next argument, #8.

How might a true civilisation perceive this?
With an ever increasing understanding of when it is best to apply competitive innovation and when it is best to apply a cooperative model of open source progression of a design/process etc. It seems to me that competition is best left to sports, entertainment and human only related work. Essentially anything that is about one human's innate abilities against another and it kept to friendly manner where the loser doesn't actually face negative consequences or threats to survival.

Cooperation seems the better option on a societal macro economic level in technical processes, design, production, manufacturing etc. where a model of a cooperative open source means of innovation seems the best approach to problem solving, taking into account equality in a democratic fashion.

Examples of this applied even within the current competitive paradigm are abundant. There have been many studies of when it has been beneficial to use a cooperative model of amateurs. The results were exceptional, like an experienced expert had worked on it[26]. The Linux operating system was made via the collaborative open source method.

Essentially, the collective intelligence trumps the individual[27]. It's common sense really, we would just need mechanisms in society to scale it up sector wide, not hinder it via data hoarding, patents, intellectual property etc.

A further brief discussion is made on this in Appendix A, under notes on themes-open source.

8. EVERY COUNTRY SHOULD JUST FOLLOW THE WESTS ECONOMIC EXAMPLE

Sample direct response

We'd need 27 planet earths by 2050 if every country lived like we do in the west!

Quick explanation of where the NLV is coming from

This is a low point for the NLV. They've recognised the level of international inequality but have shamefully blamed it on the poor, they've indirectly said the reason for global poverty is laziness or stupidity on the part of the low-income nations. It's a real ill informed argument from the NLV, which really highlights their ignorance. In my experience the NLV is actually just ignorant here not really indifferent to the plight of the poverty stricken world. The odd NLV will genuinely feel that the lazy poor dark skinned people should just get their acts together and work harder, like us white people in the west. If you find that NLV, best to leave the debate, you're basically in a discussion with a sociopath or racist, lets get the low hanging fruit first.

With the well meaning but just ignorant NLV it seems prudent to me the need to explain that the wests decadence is in direct correlation to the Global South's degradation. It's not possible for everyone to live like the west, this is the main global lie, that we can somehow raise everyone to the wests development with Sustainable Development Goals (SDG) or some other well meaning jargon on community spirit. The global game of commerce via the mechanism of exploitation through the guise of 'free' trade causes the global inequality levels and resulting poverty (more on 'freedom' in argument #13).

Poverty stricken areas rightly desire to be freed from poverty and reach the levels of material abundance the west enjoys. However, the game of free market capitalism just doesn't function like that, someone has to be the exploited in a game based on exploitation. It's simple mathematics and statistically there has to be a certain percentage of losers.

An elaboration/critique of the main point/s of the NLVs Argument

The main point however, is that it is impossible in a practical sense for everyone to live like the west does on a finite planet within an economic system so wasteful.

The Convention on Biological Diversity, the forefront of Biodiversity studies and involvement in the world, produce 5 yearly reports on the state of the global environment. In 2010 they brought in their 'Aichi Biodiversity Targets' that essentially stated: we'll be well on track to curtailing biodiversity loss by 2020 by using these 20 targets.

In their update on the targets in their November 2018 conference they conclude *'despite many positive actions by Parties and others, most of the Aichi Biodiversity Targets are not on track to be achieved by 2020, which, in the absence of further significant progress, will jeopardize the achievement of the mission and vision of the Strategic Plan for Biodiversity 2011-2020, and the Sustainable Development Goals, and ultimately the planet's life support systems'*[28].

And sure enough, in September 2020, quoting the guardians article entitled *'World fails to meet a single target to stop destruction of nature – UN report'* covering the global diversity outlook report 5 by the united nations convention on biological diversity: *'The Global Biodiversity Outlook 5, published before a key UN summit on the issue later this month, found that despite progress in some areas, natural habitats have continued to disappear, vast numbers of species remain threatened by extinction from human activities, and $500bn (£388bn) of*

*environmentally damaging government subsidies have not been
eliminated'*[29].

What's particularly funny to me is their first 'strategic goal A',
which states: *'Address the underlying causes of biodiversity loss by
mainstreaming biodiversity across government and society'.*
It's quite obvious to me what the underlying cause or root cause of
Biodiversity loss is, as I hope I've alluded to in this book and which
is abundantly explained. Basically, the core problem is the market.
Contemporary free market capitalisms structural goal is growth and
maintaining high rates of consumption. Growth in the form of
monetary profit; on a finite planet.

You gain profit through the exploitation of labour and through
consumption of natural resources. Ergo, The underlying cause of
biodiversity loss <u>IS</u> the fundamental function of our current
economic mode. It's not rocket science, but it is sacrilegious to state
that's it's the neo liberal gods fault. Especially if you're largely
operating within the deities church. Bottom line, we won't see any
improvement in biodiversity loss in this current mode nor can we
expect it to happen naturally nor for vested institutions to make any
significant change when they're submerged within the very
hegemonic overarching control mechanisms that fundamentally
counteract their goals. It is a representation of insanity.

The system does not reward or support any kind of sustainability or
efficiency of any kind. It rewards servicing, treating problems and
waste. To quote Joseph on this *'This reward/support system of
consumption in the current economic mode is now in a situation of
overshoot, where we are now consuming 2.5 Earths worth of resources
with a prediction by a study that we are on track, under a business as
usual (BAU) scenario, to need 27 planet earths by 2050 to satisfy our
consumption needs'*[30].

This contemporary form or manifestation of global waste and overshoot of earths resources is referred to as the cancer stage of capitalism, richly detailed in the illuminating book by the same name written by John McMurty. The planet is suffering from cancerous cells that grow and replicate. The cells do this under the market ideology reward system of competition, through the exploitation of scarce resources in the pursuit of individual monetary profit. This reward system operates like a game where environmental limits are an externality. Now the cancer has grown, and will continue to grow until it consumes its host in an ever-expanding function of cyclical consumption: Accumulate profit through the consumption of resources- expand- repeat.

This point of the practical impossibility of the planet to support everyone with a western lifestyle while at the same time everyone demands it is a major crux in the fundamental logic of the market. It's the main point that needs to be understood by the NLV, I hope the info above helps you pose that argument.

I find another important point that really supports this narrative is to recognise the wests material excess neurosis for what it really is: Well articulated by Joseph *The excess of the 1%...is not a condition of sound mind and intelligence but a neurotic, disrespectable condition of immaturity and irresponsibility'*... *'The drive for material excess should be seen for what it is- a sociologically driven mental illness'*

Bottom line,
Nothing will change for *any* country unless deep root changes of genuine economical reforms are incorporated, this now globalised neo-liberal god must be tackled.

Again, the question isn't what's morally right or what a well-meaning institute wishes to see change, it's a question of what works and what doesn't. Meeting environmental limits of scarcity and providing for everyone in an equal fashion is, again, just a technical question. Go to the conclusion at the end of chapter 5 for a brief discussion on this but read *'The new human rights movement'* by Peter Joseph for an in depth discussion.

The following are quick rebuttals you'd expect from an NLV in this narrative, followed by suggestions on a brief sample response.

GLOBALISATION CREATES JOBS FOR PEOPLE

Don't even dignify that with a response. After that the NLV would probably say something like *'if it wasn't for free enterprise, those kids wouldn't have jobs'*

COUNTRIES SIMPLY NEED TO DIVERSIFY THEIR ECONOMIES

Ireland for example? They added 'economic avenues'.
If every country did the despicable and shameful thing the Irish government did then yes they would be fine. However, it would then just be just a race to the bottom. If everyone relies on low/zero corporate tax to 'boost' their economy, then where does it stop?

The market ideology rewards individual profiting through the exploitation of others, so is there any wonder we have tax havens and a globalised system of tax fraud? With smaller nations 'diversifying' their economies by basically becoming the prostitutes of international finance. Not to mind the tax evasion epidemic. Wait; is it evasion or avoidance that's illegal?

IF YOU RAISE THE TAX TOO HIGH, THE RICH WILL JUST TAKE THEIR BUSINESS TO MONACO

Essentially the counterargument is the same basic argument as the above point. The problem of the global tax race to the bottom is a complex issue where, as Nicholas Shaxson, summarises in a recent article for the guardian where London is used as an example *'influential people in the UK are cheerleading for a "Singapore on the Thames" economic model after Brexit: a strategy to win the great global race to attract financial capital by lowering taxes, loosening regulations and turning a blind eye to the world's dirty money'*.

This topic would need a book of it's own to tackle, the scope of which is not within *this* book. But wait; fortunately for us there is just such a book already very eloquently written, full of detail on this elusive beast. Written by the same author of that magnificent article. *'Treasure Islands: Tax Havens and the Men who Stole the World'*, highly suggested we understand it in full, in the vain of knowing thy enemy.

Bottom line, in quick response to the NLV, I find that if you pose the 'race to the bottom' mentality argument and appeal to a noble virtue of integrity in regard to the fact the super rich are largely rich through not paying tax (community contribution). Compounded by that down right despicable threat they make to 'up and leave' (removing jobs) should they have to pay their fair share.

The same can be said about nurses, teachers and firemen 'up and leaving' if there is not a good enough public sector to support them. The argument is which society do you prefer? Full of greedy billionaires or full of great teachers, nurses and firemen?

There should be no billionaires in my opinion. A personal simple proposal I agree with- in the current mode of economics- is capping the salary ratio at 1:12 or whatever is calculated to be fair.

But again, to truly solve this problem, we need to get out of the market game and instil genuine economics. But let's move on.

THE RESOURCE CURSE IS THE PROBLEM WITH RESOURCE RICH DEVELOPING NATIONS, DIVERSIFY THE ECONOMY

No argument here. Over relying on a single resource can hinder innovation and a government needs to be diligent and protective of its economy, making sure to invest in a diversified economy with the rents from the resource to ensure a wide variety of skilled labour, very important in a global market system of competition submerged in exports and imports.

But that's the point; only in a globalised game/market system of exploitation rewarding greed, can an abundance of resources end up in more poverty and a 'curse'. It has to be one of the most blatant examples of failed logic that screams faulty fundamental system mechanics.

FINE, WELL JUST COPY SCANDINAVIAN ECONOMIES THEN!

Scandinavian economies are only successful in the global game of commerce relative to the other nations. Poverty and homelessness *do* still exist there. The state of their economy is like the middle class of a nation, you can't have the middle class without the working class and the 1% on the other side of the spectrum.

The United States is just at the most mature level of financialised capitalism; the countries that join the party get rewarded; the countries that don't get bombed back to the Stone Age.

It's abundantly more complex than that, with historical nuances etc. but the concept remains, with even 1 person living on the street or 1 child in poverty as too many. Remind the NLV of that simple point.

9. ONLY THE MARKET CAN CALCULATE THE QUANTITY OF ECONOMIC ACTIVITY IN ADVANCED INDUSTRIAL SOCIETIES

Sample direct response

T'is the lazy mans perspective. It's a cut the corner way of calculating economic activity as you don't actually calculate at all; you merely allow it to calculate itself. 'The market will calculate that through price, supply and demand' they say. Then one can merely brush off problems after the fact with jargon and the idea that: it's really complex so we couldn't have possibly predicted that outcome. The end results of this negligence are devastating effects to humanity, animals and the environment.

Quick explanation of where the NLV is coming from

The NLV is making a good point to be fair because if you are stuck in a system of classical free market capitalism with no recognition of larger order problems and novel innovations on information technology then price is the mechanism to calculate the myriad interactions; what they don't wish to accept is the negative effects and how they can be overcome with advanced computational algorithms.

So that's the point, the NLV is fixed in orthodox economics from hundreds of years ago. They don't seem to accept anything might have changed technologically that might affect that reasoning. It seems a cognitive dissonance, as they both recognise flaws yet suggest we *only* have one way of calculating economic activity, through a free market. Further, as an aside, neo-liberalism is an outgrowth of classical liberalism; it is something far more insidious and invasive than the original orthodox economics spoken of. It has not just transformed the global economic system but has set about reprogramming the socio-cultural aspects of the west in order to reinforce and legitimise the desired goal of creating a hypercompetitive individualised society that relies on isolation, fear and paranoia in an effort to negate the emergence of an alternative system.

I believe this is the main point that needs to be articulated and the major flaw in the NLV argument is that: free market capitalism is actually the lazy route to organisation, which is in contradiction to how they fashion themselves as hard working go getters. The market, in regard organisation, is a reactive, unorganised system with no proactive planning or management and doesn't have feedback on planetary sustainability.

A question on failures of sustainability or overshoot is usually followed. *'Ah, the market will calculate all that for us, no problem'*. It requires no work to manage, calculate and organise. Which leaves economists in a position of reactively assessing what happened, the whole discourse on orthodox economics is an analyse after the fact, there is no mechanism in the market to plan what should be produced, where, for who, and with no adherence to natural limits. Essentially, they don't have to calculate anything. However, we shouldn't give economists a pass here, they are just as culpable as their peers amongst moneyed and political elites. Over the last 50 years or more they have all worked in concert to bring about the current system of existence, in essence economists, especially those who came out of the Chicago and Austrian schools have developed the theory and ideology that continues to guide the development of our current model, as described in Monbiot's article in this books introduction.

It is true that in 1920 (and before) there was no mechanism to calculate all the transactions in industrial societies except for the price mechanism. But prices' failures (and the market failures in general on sustainability and overshoot) did not have a significant effect because the level of production was minimal and below what could negatively affect the planetary system.

Now however- 100 hundred years later with extremely advanced extraction and production processes, we are in a situation of drastically affecting the planetary system with the advent of technologies that produce more and more. The mechanism that calculates this activity (price) is no longer sufficient to maintain the calculations in a sustainable fashion.

So, suffice it to say as a brief reply to the impatient NLV: the pricing mechanism is obsolete; it can't calculate infinite growth capitalism efficiently enough to maintain sustainability on a finite planet. Computers *are* capable of this and are now required.

An elaboration/critique of the main point/s of the NLVs Argument

The main NLV point here is on price as a feedback mechanism. The orthodox economic idea is that price tells the entrepreneur what's needed and where. However this seems to completely disregard advertising, a huge industry devote on manipulating what is needed, where and by whom in the interests of making more profit and nothing else. Within a system where individual profit is sacrosanct and negative macro effects to the planet are not applicable then yes, price is a good means of telling them (the 'entrepreneurs') how to exploit in the best manner. But then we revert to the core argument again: that we are no longer talking about an economic system (again, in the true definition of that word) we are simply talking about a game, nothing else, of winners and losers and a finite planet being consumed in the quickest way possible. Market efficiency over technical efficiency- market economising over natural resource economising.

The tenets of *'Spontaneous order'* as proposed by Frederich Hayek in terms of economics posits that markets are a spontaneous order and price handles all the information in the background, that no human design could achieve. However, the problems with this idea are the need for an absolutely perfect reality where no coercion, manipulation or price fixing is done. Spontaneous order assumes 2 things: 1. That people act completely voluntarily, i.e there is no coercion in trade. 2. That prices are never manipulated.

This is as preposterous as is obvious, so the tenet of spontaneous order in markets as *'a more efficient allocation of societal resources than any design could achieve'* as stated by Hayek is not based on reality, only in the hypothetical. Only through a pro-active design, calculated using an equation that has no room for debate, in the same way the square root of 25 is not up for debate, can we truly have a maximum efficiency in societal resources allocation that is equitable and within environmental limits. If we don't put the calculation of environmental limits into the calculation of resource allocation then our species will inevitably consume all of them, then destroy itself; akin to a virus.

We most certainly have the capabilities of designing an efficient system that brings order in a pro-active, equitable and sustainable way. They're called Computers Frederich, they're much faster than your abacus! Although, let's be fair, he wouldn't have known the level of technology that was around the corner when he made those statements nearly 100 years ago.

Price is a way to allocate scarce resources amongst competing interests and is the intermediary between supply and demand. However, this feed back system of supply and demand is slow, inaccurate, incomplete, open for bias and, most importantly, has no mechanism inherent to calculate sustainability or scarcity. Pro-active calculations on consumption of resources are based around advertisement agencies perceived level of desires, after the fact of manipulated wants &/or needs. Basically, what you find is a system where what's on 'demand' is conjecture, a market that is slow to feed back whether that conjecture was accurate or not and compounded with an complete inability of the market to ever calculate whether that feedback was resource sustainable or not on a finite planet.

The ramifications of this lack of planning, frankly laziness, is major negative effects to global sustainably and human health. Shouldn't an 'economic' system, if you define that word correctly, be a proactive system that takes into account resource constraints and plans how to allocate them in a holistic global manner, with digital (computerised) feedback loops. This is a very difficult task, but at least we could set limits on consumption, ensuring sustainability. Maybe an appeal to the noble virtue of overcoming adversity in a cooperative manner will strike a cord with the NLV here: it's difficult, but if it was easy it wouldn't be worth doing.

The core argument essentially in contradiction to the price bias is: we can utilise technologies in a positive fashion to effectively calculate in a holistic, computer aided, real time, Internet of Things (IOT) manner where data on sustainability is inherent to the calculations, ensuring we meet earthly carrying capacity limits in real time. This attempt on a discussion around the power of information technology and the IOT to demonstrate what *could* be achieved in a genuine economy should help remove the price bias and open a good discussion on genuine economics with the NLV (Discussed previously in argument 7).

Let me quote, in summary, Josephs exemplary articulation on this: *'the IOT approach could connect and relay data regarding how best to manage resources, production processes, distribution, consumption, recycling, waste disposal behaviour, consumer demand and so on. It may seem abstract, but such a process of networked economic feedback would work on the same principle as modern systems of inventory and distribution found in major commercial warehouse... it is ultimately an issue of detail and scalability to extend this kind of awareness to all sectors of the economy, macro and micro.'...Mechanisms related to the IOT make it possible to efficiently monitor shifting consumer preference, demand, supply and labour value, virtually in real time. Moreover, IOT can be used to observe other technical processes price cannot, such as shifts in in production protocol, allocation, recycling means and so on.'*

Bottom line; the price mechanism is obsolete. Let's leave it to the orthodox economist dinosaurs.
In the next argument the NLV goes further and suggests the market doesn't need any regulation at all. Leave it completely to itself and we'll all be fine they say. Has a lazier approach ever been incorporated in history on something that has the potential to affect everyone and everything? And has/is affected/affecting everyone and everything to devastating effect.

10. JUST FREE THE MARKET COMPLETELY, GOVERNMENTS ARE THE PROBLEM

Sample direct response

'Competitive self-regulation will work out in the end. That is the façade that must be upheld, while behind the scenes large powers never play by the rules'…A 'Self regulating market economy is actually not possible in real life", through "Fraud, desperation, irrationality…the whole thing falls apart into disorder and abuse"

A perfect sample response, articulated by Joseph.

Quick explanation of where the NLV is coming from

The NLV has again recognised flaws in the market but erroneously rests those flaws solely on the shoulders of politicians and regulation by the government. This argument holds very little scientific backing as it has been tried and tested and proven to be disastrous, more of a discussion on that below. The NLV is really stuck in an archaic argument from the 50s that has managed to continue until now through jargon, double speak and question begging.

The NLV again is either complicit or ignorant. The ignorant NLV is probably just towing the line of right wing jargon and doesn't really understand (or hasn't researched) the ramifications of de-regulation on a macro scale. They've probably read an article that gives a micro example of when government red tape resulted in a negative and then accepted the argument 'governments are bad, umkay'. Again, very typical of an NLV, no critical thinking required.

The complicit NLV here is actually quite dangerous, especially if they are quite well read, charming and articulate. In this instance though, they've also reached a macro conclusion from a micro example. They, however, have presumably done the research yet do not reason that something must be done to control the devastating outcomes of 'liberal' markets. One can only conclude they are happy to sacrifice people for what they believe is a long-term benefit (also discussed below) *or* quite simply: they are socio-paths.

This argument is usually preceded by micro examples of systemic flaws, for example: *'my coffee shop can't grow because there's too much paper work....'* or by simple statements on how inefficient the public sector is compared to how super efficient a market would be without red tape holding it back: *'the public sector is a bunch of thumb twiddlers waiting for their pension...'.*

The public sector uses the carrot to coerce people to work while the private sector uses the stick. When you're threatened with survival, people will work to whatever standard the stick demands.

The NLVs core argument here is to allow the stick to do as it wishes without any control. One would hope common sense would prevail here against the idea that unfettered market corrections on labour with corporations doing as they see fit to the environment would be disastrous and *has* been disastrous.

The response then to their core argument: Corporations are *already* running a muck, destroying the planet and subjugating millions to horrible working conditions, and this is with our best efforts to control them. The micro necessities on business - like government forms and inspections- are a cost; but a most necessary cost in the effort to control the macro throes of corporation's hell bent on maximising profit through the exploitation of labour and natural resources. Further, How can they not run wild when they can sue countries and are now considered to have the same rights as humans in courts?[31]

I believe the NLV just needs reassuring on the fact this cost is a requirement when we have an economic system based on competition, exploitation and individual profit pursuit through constant consumption on a finite planet.

An elaboration/critique of the main point/s of the NLVs Argument

The core concept that must be understood here is that corporations have instilled an ideology to ensure they go unfettered on their pursuit of profit. The larger a business gets, the more it can abuse labour globally, purchase government leniency, evade tax and push costs onto the environment. Large corporations never play by the rules; they are not programmed to do so, within the rules framed by the very core of the economic mode. The ideology of completely free markets, or so called laissez faire economics has been experimented on before and *'Not surprisingly, this market fundamentalism, closer to theology than economic reality, also failed'*, Eric Hobsbawn describing how this completely laissez faire market ideology, or theology, also failed alongside the socialist fundamentalists of early soviet Russia[32.]

Hobsbawn's research confirms the example of the economic ideologies pursued by Milton Friedman and the Chicago school of economics during their 'experiments' in South America through the late decades of the 20th century[33]. Not the scope here to detail the outcomes of those experiments, I assume the reader is aware of the brutal military juntas. The reference given gives a great summary example, further reading abundant, most notably by Noam Chomsky or Amartya Sen.

However, what Hobsbawn means is that it failed as a system, in that poverty is still rife and *'capitalism was by its nature incapable of framing the subsequent economy of social production'*. What did succeed however was probably precisely what the adherents of neo-liberalism were gunning for and essentially what the system encourages them to do, i.e. a complete concentration of wealth, self profit with complete disregard for everything else. With 8 people in control of the same amount of wealth as half the global population today, a resounding success is actually the pertinent conclusion?

The core market game incentive: maximise individual monetary profit and disregard everything else. That disregard is now at a devastating effect. 'Left' government policy is an effort to control the negative outgrowths of that pursuit. Political parties like the labour party in the UK, were at their origins created to counter the negative outcomes of that pursuit for profit through the exploitation of labour. Political parties like 'the greens' are an attempt to counter the negative outcomes of that pursuit for profit through the exploitation of the environment. Where the various 'left' parties through the world are aligned now is another topic and the core of it is discussed in argument #13.

Where we can see today that it is only an *attempt* by well meaning 'left' politicians, as we can see in modern politics; a party or politician does not rise to prominence if it/he/she does not align with the interests of business, especially that of the dictates of big business. In reality; modern 'democratic' governments are essentially business governments, with the interests of the largest businesses a priority. Anyway, this very important topic is discussed further in argument #13.

The point here though is the fact of corporations running amuck and completely disregarding social, health and environmental concerns in their pursuit for profit. 'Left' governments are merely another hurdle that needs to be bought-out, so they can continue in their pursuits unhindered; everything is for sale. We have seen the level of monetary accusation fervour and avarice people caught up in this game reach. However, these people are just nodes in a system designed to profit and disregard negative outcomes. Corporations therefore are a beast of their own and can only be controlled by concerted regulation. There has been no success in this regard though really and they continue to grow, exploit across borders and expand their influence. The NLV has somehow been brainwashed to encourage this, which is actually in detriment to themselves- Cultural hegemony as discoursed by Antonio Gramsci, alluded to before.

The root problem is the rules of the game itself, corporations are just agents programmed to act in a certain way. The 'right', like the techno capitalist apologists, believe it will all work out in the end; the meek suffer what they must for the good of the species. The 'left' believe it is a moral problem and if we just had a few more carrots, a few more forms and a few more safety nets then corporations would stop behaving like they do and we'd all be fine. An example being the effort to raise the living wage or get money out of politics, this is like asking water not to be wet; profiting through the exploitation of labour and purchasing government leniency (lobbying) is just how the market functions at its core. Corporations are merely acting as rewarded to do so.

Briefly, let me make a distinction here between the "new left" as in the neoliberalised Blairite left that emerged in the 90s and self-styled "postmodern leftists" who are more concerned with mezzo issues such as gender, sexuality and ethnicity, these two groups retreated from economic based class politics and left the field open for the entry of populist right wing politicians like Donald Trump and Boris Johnson. Whereas now, possibly, we are beginning to see a return to more traditional left wing issues under the likes of Bernie Sanders and Jeremy Corbyn, even though both have been unsuccessful never the less they have brought traditional left wing ideals back to the forefront.

This response is essentially the core of globalised corporations masquerading under the guise of 'freedom' to maximise their own freedom to profit (through the subjection of others), this will be discussed in chapter 3, argument #14.

Both the left and the right in modern society try to treat symptoms; rarely do they try to cure the root disease. The solution is eradicating the root mechanisms that encourage and reward corporations to seek profit at all costs. The root problem and a discussion on genuine economics are discussed in chapter 5.

The following is a quick rebuttal you'd expect at some stage in the discussion from an NLV, followed by a suggested brief sample response.

SOCIAL WELFARE PROGRAMS MAKE PEOPLE LAZY

This can only be true in a capitalistic society based on exploitation where the outputs of the market produce poverty. In response the left try to alleviate this negative output by giving people fish and not teaching them how to fish; rightly we can agree that it will have a negative outcome. Teaching people how to fish is always a better approach, in a macro economic example, some African nations refuse IMF loans and work to solve their own poverty problems, the results have been better in the long run[34].

We're essentially talking about solutions to the negative outcomes in the system. Social welfare programmes are a way to alleviate the suffering. The symptoms of the current system are deadly; we can't allow people to suffer with our indifference. The true solution is not patchwork to the wound (social welfare programs) nor is it burning the wound closed (more deregulated free market corrections for the poor).

The solution is to stop creating the wound in the first place. Basically a new system altogether, that doesn't produce poverty in the first place. Again, one person living in the street is too many. So continuing a system that constantly has a certain percentage of people on the street is not the solution. Nor is chucking money at them hoping they'll go away. A brief description of a genuine economic system is posed in the conclusion of this book and in Appendix A.

11. PHILANTHROPY FROM BILLIONAIRES WILL EVENTUALLY FIX CAPITALISMS FLAWS

Sample direct response
Half the world suffers in poverty and it's growing. Poverty is an inherent flaw in contemporary capitalism, people only have billions of dollars through the core functions of contemporary capitalism, namely exploiting labour and resources. Being a billionaire is in direct correlation to poverty. So, you hope to solve poverty with the very mechanism that produces it? This is just silly.

Quick explanation of where the NLV is coming from
This is an argument by an exceptionally well brainwashed-NLV. They've seen the excesses of billionaires and believe everyone can be like that if they just apply themselves, they see billionaires as the most intelligent and the only ones that could possibly solve these terrible 'natural' problems and flaws in human 'nature'. The argument recognizes inherent flaws in the current system but performs mental gymnastics and doesn't envisage how billionaires got to be billionaires in the first place, which is the reason the NLV doesn't see that trying to solve poverty with the very mechanism that produces it is insanity.

Again we have 2 types of NLV.
The majority is just ignorant of the complexities of global market capitalism. The complicit ones are the actual millionaires & billionaires, who genuinely believe they can sort out these 'natural' global problems using their exceptional wealth *or* they just say that to keep us quiet. Complicity ignorant or just complicit megalomaniacs.

The ignorant NLV is where we will focus our discussion here; not much point arguing with a complicit billionaire. Trying to ask them to use their wealth to instill functions in society that would remove billionaires seems just as silly as the argument itself. Would be like asking the neo-liberal god to abdicate. Billionaires are. I'm sure, really intelligent people, (or are they intelligent or are they just very cunning opportunistic predators?) makes sense for that level of wealth in this competitive game, but I think bubble mentality comes into play and -on average -a lack of empathy, compounded by how they got to be billionaires in the first place. One study comes to mind where people played monopoly against each other, one person was given extreme advantages from the outset and on average felt they deserved to win because of their superior skills &/or intelligence[35].

There are already currently mechanisms to support everyone in the current system, if the wealth was just distributed fairly. Jeffrey Sachs, as one of the world's leading experts on economic development and the fight against poverty, calculated the cost to end poverty is $175 billion per year for 20 years[36]. However if we were to incorporate and apply our best available technologies to their fullest potential we would not only remove poverty but also greatly increase the standard of living for the vast majority of people on the planet. The 0.1% already have everything they need/want by the way, at the expense of everyone else, they will just never give it up, it is simply counter intuitive to the core functions of the ideology of markets. There is no incentive or historical reason to think otherwise.

A major problem will be that the elites are now too powerful and will allow a lot of suffering before giving up the power. One can imagine all sorts of riots against the police as climate refugees flood the not-currently affected countries.

Concurrently, the ignorant NLV assumes the *only* reason billionaires are billionaires are because of their exceptional intelligence. Further they believe anyone can be a billionaire if they are intelligent enough. The problem with their point of view is the word *ONLY; in* their ignorance they completely disregard the myriad wealth concentrating functions of a rigged economic system that is structurally violent and oppressive.

The core rebuttal is simple to the ignorant NLV then: it is not possible for everyone to become a billionaire, first because there just isn't enough resources to satisfy that level of material excess (as discussed in argument #7) and second; because they are only billionaires through the functions of globalised financial free market capitalism, their intelligence is only one attribute of a myriad of variables to combine to create billionaires. Most importantly: a rigged economic system that favours and concentrates wealth. The problems that billionaires tackle through their philanthropy are not *natural, produced by mother-nature* nor are they *produced naturally through human nature.* They are manmade problems created by the inherent gaming logic of contemporary financial free market capitalism.

Bottom line, the simple counter argument is which society do you prefer? Full of greedy billionaires or full of great teachers, nurses and firemen?

The NLV will usually then adamantly state, *'it's great to have billionaires, it gives us all focus and inspiration to strive for greatness',* this core concept has already been discussed in argument numbers 5 through 7 and could be reiterated.

An elaboration/critique of the main point/s of the NLVs Argument

To elaborate on the main point, being: the assumption that the problems that billionaires tackle through their philanthropy are 'natural, produced by Mother Nature or are produced naturally through human 'nature'.

The counter argument is that the problems we tackle are manmade and a question on how are they 'rich' in the first place sets it up? The answer is through -on average, exceptions aside – labour and resource exploitation, fraud, evasion &/or avoidance of tax, lobbying, purchasing policy (crony capitalism) and so on. These routes to wealth acquisition are all part of the gaming logic of modern markets. This gaming logic results in vast inequality, hence poverty, hence violence. These are all created by the inherent gaming logic of contemporary financial free market capitalism through the commandments of the neo-liberal god. Requesting the resulting winners of the game to fix the negative outputs of the game, in complete detriment to the very logic of how they were rewarded is extremely illogical, if not insane.

An exemplary point on how corporations reach exceeding wealth and then individuals become billionaires through exploitation is the fact that no company would be profitable if full calculations on negative effects on the environment were incorporated into the calculation[37] as calculated in a report titled 'Natural Capital at Risk: the Top 100 externalities of Business' by an environmental consultancy Trucost on behalf of The Economics of Ecosystems and Biodiversity (TEEB) program sponsored by United Nations Environmental Program. The report showed how total ecological damage in the top 5 sectors has a more drastic economic effect on the environment as can be profitable to them, as per table illustrated below (Table 2). The key point here is that these are considered 'externalities', people get extremely wealthy by exploiting the environment (and other humans) and the cost is dumped on mother nature and the rest of us. But again, this is just a core function of

how our current game of markets function (our so called
'economy').

RANK	SECTOR	REGION	NATURAL CAPITAL COST, $BN	REVENUE, $BN	IMPACT RATIO
1	COAL POWER GENERATION	EASTERN ASIA	452.8	443.1	1.0
2	CATTLE RANCHING AND FARMING	SOUTH AMERICA	353.8	16.6	18.8
3	COAL POWER GENERATION	NORTHERN AMERICA	316.8	246.7	1.3
4	WHEAT FARMING	SOUTHERN ASIA	266.6	31.8	8.4
5	RICE FARMING	SOUTHERN ASIA	235.6	65.8	3.6

Table 1: top five industrial sectors ranked by total ecological damages imposed.

The game of markets rewards avarice, greed and indifference to your competitors (everyone else). On average the more your personality suits these traits the more 'successful' you will be.

Billionaires like Bill Gates setting up the bill gates foundation and doing great work in the world should most certainly be commended and congratulated for giving back. But giving back is just that; giving *back*. An acceptance that they have *taken* in the first place, it's recognition that only through market functionality of competitive gaming resulting in inequality can there be a billionaire. Billionaires giving back is a recognition that they don't know how to solve the core market problems producing brutal poverty in the first place.

However, what we find are billionaires giving back and stating that they will continue to do so until they resolve all these negative outcomes we suffer. However they could remove poverty globally with their own profits quite easily. The 175 Billion USD a year, calculated by Sachs in his book discussed above, could be paid by the estimated 2,153 billionaires there currently are in the world as shown in Forbes 2020 Billionaire list[38]. But they won't, because that would be completely outside the neo-liberal gods commandments and would basically result in a change in how the system functions, the same system that rewarded them so generously.

So the core problem with NLVs argument here is the conflation between these 2 points:

1.) Billionaires giving back and
2.) Billionaires giving back but stating that we shouldn't fundamentally change the negative functions of a flawed market system because billionaires will solve it.

This conflation by the NLV is a drastic leap in reality, extremely naive and could have very damaging effects. Through their ignorance they encourage a system of poverty creation and would happily rest the power to solve this devastating output in the hands of the most rewarded by the very system that produced the problem in the first place. This is quite dangerous, as suggested before, as a complicit NLV here is usually very intelligent and articulate etc.

An important thing to note here is that the richer people get the less they give as a percentage to their wealth[39] and they tend to give back through donations to what would be perceived as 'middle class' concerns, i.e. scientific research or university programmes. Not on direct alleviation of poverty. It seems they want to keep their money in the club as it were, on average, and donations are usually related to tax write offs[40].

12. SOMEBODY HAS TO DO THE UNDESIRABLE WORK

Sample direct response

That's really a question of values, are you happy to live in a society of exploitation, if so, stop what you're doing and become a stockmarketeer. But you have to notice in society today, the more undesirable the work is, the further it is down the social ladder, people are looked down on for serving us, picking up our rubbish, cleaning etc. while people that play a game or pretend to be someone else- like football players or an actor, arguably the easiest jobs, are held up the highest and paid the most. It should be directly opposite no? Those undesirable jobs are the most *arduous* _and_ *most required.*

Quick explanation of where the NLV is coming from

It's a foundational argument again used in response to questions on how a system of control is required to keep people working also used in response to questions on the drastic difference between how arduous one type of job is to another and who needs to do these tough jobs.

This argument is usually preceded by *'we have to coerce people into work because…'* or *'If we didn't have a controlling system people would just lie on the couch all day watching Jeremy Kyle…'*

The free market system requires x % of people to be worker drones, it's institutions have been incorporated and continue to function in that fashion, however well-meaning they may presume to be. It will always regress to that singular line of maximising exploitation of labour to minimise costs hence maximise profits. Asking our current 'economic' mode to not exploit labour is basically like asking water not to be wet.

Does it not speak volumes for how deplorable this modern form of 'economics' has become in that we need to presume human nature is at its core lazy. So the only manner to advance the species is a system of control, coercion and threats to survival. The argument assumes humans would simply stop living if we didn't threaten or coerce them. That's quite offensive I find.

One finds pride in work, when craftsmen can work themselves, when they finish it they know what its for, get direct reward etc. money is abstract and removes the finished product from the producer. It leaves us humans without a sense of agency; a human without a purpose is what creates this assumption of laziness. This has been discussed in argument #4 however so let's not belabor the point. And a discussion on the need for humans to have a vocation, not a 'job' (as described in argument #5) will be discussed more in argument #19.

But suffice it to state the simple point here: undesirable work is necessary but we are left with 2 options in our current mode of 'economics'; we either have wage slaves or we share it out. They're our options, which would you prefer?

A 3rd option, within free market capitalism, is: Could we have a system that paid very well for doing those undesired jobs? That's not reality however; it's the exact opposite and will always be so. That idea goes head-on in contradiction with the neo-liberal gods commandments of profit through exploitation, this would be a most hennas sacrilege and in my opinion; impossible.

The best option: have a genuine economic system that strives to minimise the quantity of monotonous/arduous labour through automation and maximises the value of doing work that can't be automated. The most arduous automated first.

An elaboration/critique of the main point/s of the NLVs Argument

A high standard of living should not have to correlate with exploitation and coercion where the coerced live unhealthy, unhappy lives. A rigged system that siphons the wealth upwards, further concentrating the further it goes up will result in this.

In contrast, the standard of living should exactly correlate to what we can provide as a society without exploiting, coercing or forcing people into unhealthy and unhappy lives. With a new form of society based on collaboration, altruism within environmental limits we would have a root socioeconomic orientation that would- as if by an invisible hand- remove those unwanted jobs gradually until they are fully automated. Pun intended.

One can imagine an exponential scale, where at the start there is a high quantity of man-hours required for the undesirable work with the goal to minimise this in whatever way possible. Note; these jobs usually require little to no skill or training (hence the undesiredness, as they are antithetical to human mental functionality) so they could be shared evenly amongst the able peoples in that community and automated first. Imagine every person required to do something they don't like every week for 2 hours at an ever-decreasing scale until it is fully automated.

Wouldn't everyone work or at the very least be highly interested in seeing technologies that can free them of it? Historically looking at humanities pace at which it solves problems that are known and desired to be solved by all: One can imagine full mechanisation of all repetitive, dehumanising, boring jobs in a matter of years.

Noting the difference of jobs to vocations: I like to do gardening for example; when we reach full automation, I will continue to do it; exemplary of the rebuttal to the core argument.

The core NLV counter argument here is that hating work is part of capitalism, as you don't gain satisfaction or direct reward, the factory line nature of it removes the homo-sapiens nature to create. The factory line ethos essentially creates a general zeitgeist of people vexed with their work because they simply can't do their work well and don't get the feeling of being fulfilled or prideful with a finished product.

Humans standing in a factory line in the 21st century with the level of technology we have is simply negligent and offensive. A perfect example of this are labourers at a waste transfer station picking line; 8 hours per day with loud machines and ear muffs just standing there, not talking to anyone, picking material off a conveyor belt and throwing it into a particular bin. Mind-numbing to say the least but offensive to evolution and negligent to potentials in automation. The work is currently abundantly necessary but I say not at the cost of our humanity.

Granted, an incentive system is definitely beneficial and dare I say required but when you cross that line of incentive to coercion with threats to survival we cross that line into inhumanity. Competition as a mechanism for a labour incentive certainly has its plus sides but most certainly it's negatives also, as can be seen today in its modern socio-economic form: Sweat shops, child labour etc.

An example for simplicity:
A losing football team has 4 good players. You can't say the team is a good team just on those 4. The team is losing, as a whole therefore the team is a poor team.

Assume competition has 11 attributes. You can't say competition works just because 4 attributes are beneficial and the rest devastatingly negative. The current form of competition through exploitation and a coercive work ethic is a poor incentive system.

Again, A more detailed discussion on how humans need a vocation in life, not a 'job' (as described in argument #5), will be discussed more in argument #19.

The following are quick rebuttals you'd expect from an NLV in this narrative, followed by suggestions on a brief sample response.

IT WILL BE TOO INEFFICIENT AS WE WOULD NEED TO TRAIN EVERYONE TO DO EVERY JOB

Most people can learn rudimentary jobs in an hour. If a person is not adept enough to do even these jobs then they shouldn't be working at all. Society should have this minimum meagre level of integrity not to require these incapable people to work; this tiny fraction of people would be just looked after.

BUT PEOPLE HAVE DIFFERENT TALENTS, WHY WOULD A DOCTOR SWEEP ROADS??

Initially that makes sense, but an historical systemic perspective must be taken on the doctor and the road sweepers lives?
If Einstein was born and raised in a slum, the chances of him becoming the genius he became are incredibly minimised.
So although, its correct to say a doctor *now* shouldn't be sweeping roads, a system that increasingly spreads evenly undesired work, while giving everyone equal opportunities will produce an

equitable distribution with a system of profiting from individuals talents.

If everyone is allowed to pursue his or her area of interest/talent without coercion or force then everybody will be 'above' road sweeping and it would be shared equitable until all arduous monotonous jobs are automated. Note how easily it is to automate these roles.

Again, an adaptive system is key. Whatever works; works! Make a system that strives to minimise the quantity of monotonous/arduous labour and maximises the value of doing work, looking to automate first the most arduous.

Succinctly, the economic system that neo-liberalism espouses, agrees nicely with the politics of dominance & control. The more poverty stricken people are the less they have the ability to engage in the overall system, they are simple too busy just trying to survive. On a graph we would see two lines coupled, as poverty rises, political engagement falls. The economic systems of progressives need an engaged populous, hence they need poverty alleviated so people can have the time and resources to engage. It's essentially a vicious cycle and no wonder we have right politics generally dominant in an economic system that produces that level of inequality, hence poverty.

A solution to the poverty problem is one of assessment of resources and equal distribution globally, claiming all of earth's resources as common heritage. The pragmatics of that on a global scale is another question but the concept is simple. To re-iterate, only in the current mode of our species interaction with the environment do we have these vast levels of poverty, only in a system where scarcity is the rule, does scarcity remain the curse. Apply technology to maximise abundance within planetary limits, essentially, a true economic system, in the truest sense of the word.

'By the end of 2020, economists expect global debt to reach $277 trillion, or 365% of world GDP' gives further credence to the functions of international finance and the neo-liberal ideology that supports it[41]. Who's in debt to whom? The global level of poverty is not going anywhere while a dominant ideology that basically produces it exists. Only a globalised system of equality, quantification of resources and equal distribution of them will alleviate poverty.

Localisation instead of globalisation is a good step in that direction, a brief discussion on that in Appendix A.

Being an NLV, well; just a right-winger in general or a tow-the-line journalist requires little to no use of facilities of critical thinking in socioeconomics or politics. One merely reads some standard discourse, tow the status quo argument and you'll be praised, on average. I find it both heartening and disheartening at the same time. It's disheartening that there is such a VAST quantity of our species that lack the capability or gumption for simple critical analysis, or maybe rather they do possess it but are satisfied with their sufficiently comfortable cage they've been given for their obedience... is that any better though? Is it really their fault though, when for several generations we have been fed a cultural diet that exhorts the value of consumption, and has systematically eroded the value of art and cultural expression?

What's heartening in contrast I suppose is the fact that it's the truly intelligent, ambitious, critical thinkers then that dominate the 'left'; eventual victory seems an evitable outcome with a more enduring in depth approach to civilised society. But, maybe I'm too optimistic, the left is still fractured into at least 3 camps: Neoliberal (Blarite) Left, Postmodern Left and Traditional Class Politics Left. See Appendix A for a brief critique of todays left in my opinion.

In the next chapter we will discuss the fallacies of modern day democracy, freedom and what private property really means. Can we really have 'freedom' in a system of coercion? Where just about everything is bought and sold, even government policy. In a system of competition wouldn't that then mean one person's freedom is another's subjection? Can we truly have democracy submerged in a system of vast inequality? Vote with your dollar they say? Isn't a billionaires' vote worth more than mine then?

CHAPTER 3: MY DEMOCRACY, MY FREEDOM, MY PROPERTY

"WAR is a racket. It always has been. It is possibly the oldest, easily the most profitable, surely the most vicious. It is the only one international in scope. It is the only one in which the profits are reckoned in dollars and the losses in lives."
— General Smedley D. Butler, War Is a Racket

It's hard to fathom how the words 'Freedom and democracy' have been so brutally bastardised by the current power structures. It really boggles the mind how this blatant double speak is used to gain control and pursue ventures in the interests of profit in the name of democracy and freedom. Freedom really means exploitation and instigating democracy really means installing a dictator, as history as shown numerous times[42]. This tentacle of the established system has somehow infected the group mind, analogous to a cult brainwashing.
Details will be provided in this chapter but if you've just read this and are saying 'what are you talking about man' then put this book down and read anything by Noam Chomsky immediately to understand the true functions of modern power in the name of freedom and democracy, of note; the book 'hegemony or survival'.

What is quite encouraging to understand however is that the powers that be don't simply run riot & proclaim they are doing as such, we are now at the level where they must lie and deceive; as they've come to understand that it now won't be tolerated. Exploitation of a country for it's natural resources in the 21st century can no longer be done overtly. The use of linguistic gymnastics is required: 'These people are terrorists and they require our freedom and democracy', follow this by a shock to the day-to-day lives and you have acceptance by the masses, allowing the 'liberators' to go aplunderin' unabated. Naomi Klien has exceptionally publicized this use of shocks in her book 'the shock doctrine', leaving one to question a 'terrorist attack' as really a false flag[43].

The take-away here, nobody can be trusted to tell you the truth in a system that has at its core competition, exploitation and domination. They use and have used every trick in the book to secure their share (unfairly resulting) of resources. Be it from neighbourhood to neighbourhood or country to country (a.k.a gangs and war). Manifestations are abundant, all encompassing and deadly. If you can agree with that simple point, which only requires looking out the window for justification, then it is no leap to link the fact that democracy is shrouded in connivance, trickery, underhandedness and coercion, 'Freedom' merely another tool used by people with 'all the tools' to secure more wealth. Freedom and democracy, in the truest sense of the words, are impossible in free market capitalism.

My patience is wearing thin with the hypocrisy, I can't watch the TV without cringing, read the paper without sighing, listen to the radio with out a 'tut'. This cancerous disease: free market capitalism and it's driver neo-liberalism, has found itself in the perfect environment to proliferate and is now getting out of control, it's no longer acceptable to allow more people to become brainwashed and fall prey to the very people that are victimising them. The shroud must be blown back and illuminated for its true essence.

To this end I humbly wish to present some common arguments I've encountered in the past in protection of 'democracy' and 'freedom' and give some sample direct responses followed by a more detailed critique of the flaw in the argument. Understanding a full concept is best achieved by the ability to explain it to yourself in metaphor. Therefore, during conversation with an NLV, we can find ourselves with the ability to bespoke the response, below are just samples I've personally come across. *'Capture their hearts and the mind will follow'*.

13. BE LIKE THE WEST, IN THE WEST WE HAVE DEMOCRACY

Sample direct response

Democracy for who? Are the bottom rungs of society really represented? If they were would they really accept those conditions?

If we were to have a pure democratic system, then the reality of 1% of people owning 50% of the wealth would be impossible. There's nothing democratic about our system today.

Quick explanation of where the NLV is coming from

I believe the point the NLV makes here is only really relative to other authoritarian governments or to historical dictatorship-type governments. Propaganda has manipulated them sufficiently to have them believe that western democracies are fully functional and working correctly because: 'look how little democracy they got der in CHINA'. Then the propagandist would merely repeat 'China' a few times followed by a couple of 'terrorists' and top it off with a little 'Nazi', resulting in a sufficiently placated and accepting NLV for 'our democracy' in the west. Essentially the point from the NLV is reductive and frankly pathetic, it is the argument that things have been worse for democracy before therefore 'you better be happy with what you got'. Essentially, having a poorly functioning democratic system doesn't matter because it could be a lot worse. This is just negligent, unhelpful and really just feeds into the common framework of keeping us divided and pitted against each other.

The NLV has a fundamental belief here on the efficacy of democracy, we need to present the fact that modern democracy is a hierarchical representative system, although there are voters; it is still top down which suits perfectly to the core functions of

capitalism; namely, control and domination. This however is in complete contradiction to what democracy actually means. True democracy cannot function with capitalism, it only means democracy for the owners of capital, not everyone and it's that simple. What results is little to no real agency on ones own life and the illusion of a say in affairs. To quote Slavoj Žižek in 1989 *"That is to say, democracy always entails the possibility of corruption, of the rule of dull mediocrity, the only problem is that every attempt to elude this inherent risk and to restore 'real' democracy necessarily brings about its opposite -it ends in the abolition of democracy itself"*
How do we square an allegedly benevolent democracy that caters to the needs of the many without allowing it to be corrupted and realigned to cater to the needs of the few due to it being submerged in a economic system that encourages and rewards it to do so?

The major flaw in contemporary representative democracy is that you end up just voting between just 2 parties or even just between 2 personalities, where half the time the vote is usually just to prevent someone else or a particular policy or event. Case in point is the 2018 UK general elections. The vote went for the conservative party where a multitude of labour/working class constituencies voted conservative instead. This change can really be attributed to a number of factors- lack of understanding on where there true economic inequality problems lie, right wing blatant lies and/or propaganda to divide the poor against immigrants- but what seems obvious is that a large contributing factor was their vote for a 'strong Brexit deal' and an assumption that *'Corbyn is not a strong enough leader to get us away from those Europeans who are stealing all our money and making all our rules'* (paraphrase of NLV #18435). So they voted to stop labour because they had been sufficiently brainwashed to believe only the conservatives can get a strong Brexit deal. What results is: this form of 'democracy' did not/could not take into account their needs for equal pay, a reduction in inequality, more social housing, health care, education etc.

If you're looking for an in-depth scientific analysis of this and an illumination on the fact that contemporary democracy essentially means the ability to vote between a giant douche and a third sandwich; see the T.V series; 'South park', season 8, episode 8. Obviously I'm being facetious, to emphasis the fact that it's really not complicated at all. Adorno and Hokheimer, writing in the 30s and 40s, prophesied the emergence of a collation of entities within the entertainment/culture industry and the state and capitalist elites that in essence was and still is designed to promote their combined ideologies and negate the ability to truly think of an alternative[44].

No part of the power structures in 'democratic' countries could be considered 'true' democracy and the fanfare of voting between two particular career politicians at any given time is a complete farce, especially in the abundantly more complicated society of the 21st century in comparison to when these archaic systems began.

Vote with your dollar they say, so a billionaire has a billion votes and Joe blogs has none. The 'democratic' system in modern capitalistic societies simply can't provide a means for everyone to have equal say. If it did the whole thing would fall apart. People would vote for what they needed most, not just a particular current affair and the 1% would lose their control completely. Capitalism is based on control and dominance, democracy means equal say; It's an oxymoron, a contradiction in terms. Remind the NLV of that.

An elaboration/critique of the main point/s of the NLVs Argument

The core counterargument here is that corrupt governments are a natural outgrowth of the economic mode. They have and always will function as a regulatory structure to maintain the interests of the dominant class, or in the cases of western democracies: whoever has the most amount of money to influence the votes. Expecting a government to be morally good in a system submerged and constructed for them to be competitive, dominating, individualistic etc. will only *and* inevitably produce the corruption you see today. Crony capitalism is like bread and butter; the well-meaning activists asking for money to be out of politics are naive.

Peter Joseph inserted a paragraph into his book, written by economist John C. Wood, providing a summary of the work of Thorsten Veblen, arguably the foremost intellectual on this topic of capitalism's gravitation or inherent nature for 'crony capitalism'. I can find no better an example that succinctly summarises this completely neglected- yet extremely important- part of society. In the interest of presenting what I feel is the finest summary of Veblen's work on the topic and not reinventing the wheel, allow me to quote John C Wood again. I quote this safe with the knowledge that the concise nature of it should provide you the tools required to effectively refute the NLV in this regard:

'Veblen wrote extensively and insightfully on the relations between capitalist government and the class struggle. For Veblen, the ultimate power in the capitalistic government is in the hands of the owners because they control the government. The government is the institutionally legitimising means of physical coercion in any society. As such, it exists to protect the existing social order and class structure. This means the primary role of government is to enforce private property laws and protect the privilege associated with ownership. Veblen repeatedly insisted that "modern politics is business politics…" the first principle of a capitalistic government (to quote Veblen) "the natural freedom of the individual must not traverse the prescriptive rights of property. Property rights…have the indefeasibility which attached to natural rights." The principle freedom of capitalism is the freedom to buy and sell. The laissez faire philosophy dictates that (to quote Veblen) "so long as there is no overt attempt on life…or liberty to buy and sell, the law cannot intervene, unless it be in a

precautionary way to prevent prospective violation of...property rights."
Thus above all else (to quote Veblen) " a constitutional government is a
business government."

The core function of contemporary capitalistic society, now global
in scope, is to maximise individual profit. This is done through
corporations; governments are merely tools in the goal of profit
seeking to legitimise the coercive requirements. Coercion is
required because nobody is going to accept the level of exploitation
required to attain those profits as maximising profits means
minimising labour rights as a function of 'what can we get away
with'. Governments therefore act as a *'legitimising means of physical
coercion'* to ensure labour is coerced in a profitable manner and
business (profits) continue to grow unchecked. Contemporary
democratic governments are then just business governments.

The needs of the many are not part of the equation in the
overarching interest of the controlling mechanism and maturations
of big business. The needs of the many then are merely by-products
of the goal of profiteering where an understanding that an
oppressive equilibrium must be maintained, in that: too much
oppression and labour will revolt and too little labour coercion and
there will be a loss of profit.

To conclude in a sentence: the role of government- at a core level
submerged in a capitalistic system- is one of ensuring profit can be
achieved unhindered by business and ones 'private' property rights
are always respected and protected, also to secure competitive
advantage for the largest businesses that fund and basically control
them. These are the commandments of the neo liberal god and are
sacrosanct. Democracy, in definition, is just an illusion. The only
democracy that exists is business democracy.

In argument #14 we discuss the quote above in more detail: *"The principle freedom of capitalism is the freedom to buy and sell".*

14. BE LIKE THE WEST, IN THE WEST WE HAVE OUR FREEDOM

Sample direct response

Individually: freedom is only what your purchasing power allows you. Internationally: freedom means the freedom for business to do whatever it wants, which is always at the subjugation of others. Business can only profit through exploitation.

Quick explanation of where the NLV is coming from

The main argument here by the NLV is usually posed as a response or justification for the vast inequality on the global scale. This reaction usually comes when the NLV needs to justify that the suffering is ok simply because the people of the poorer nations don't know how to organise themselves, if they would just follow the wests shining free market example they would be fine.

It's essentially a display of extreme arrogance, intolerance and ignorance. The arrogance is of western ego-centrism; the intolerance of other cultures (projecting morals) and the ignorance is of the multi-faceted nuances of geo politics. In typical NLV fashion everything is reduced to a single point and can be assessed on abstraction with some foundational belief that the neo-liberal god has instilled. It's usually posed after some terrible display of corruption or atrocity in a developing nation. It needs immediate challenging because a group of NLVs will then usually build it into racism of some form, while obviously not condoning the corruption or atrocity but framing it correctly (discussed below further).

The basic NLV argument here that can be quickly refuted is the conflation between the freedoms they spout and what freedom actually means. They've been sufficiently brainwashed to think the freedom they have to *choose* a job, *choose* a house and *choose* a certain car means complete freedom to do as they wish without coercion, manipulation and everything or interaction is voluntary.

'Free trade' as discussed in orthodox economic circles is/was a laissez faire idea, in that somehow we are completely free of coercion with all agents in the competitive game of commerce acting with full agency, voluntarily, free of coercion or manipulation resulting in *'spontaneous order'*, as developed by Frederich Hayek nearly 80 years ago, origins with Adam Smith and his famous invisible hand maxim some 200 years ago.

Nothing could be further from the truth, the emphasis on 'choose' above was intentional. Each of these 'free' *choices* are perfect examples of institutionalised points of *limits on choice*, where starting from birth, your social status and position in society has direct and over arching effects on everything you have *options* on purchasing. Your purchasing power is fully affected by your advantages, disadvantages and mostly luck in the competitive gaming logic of the market. Freedom, without coercion, simply does not exist with a systemic perspective in a social system submerged in the logic of domination and exploitation. It's a basic oxymoron.
In this game, the logic is apt that one person's liberty is another's subjugation. Think of the highly educated migrant waiting tables.

Trying to get an NLV to see the conflation and the motive of the establishment to have that conflation instilled in the masses I find a difficult task in my experience. An analogy as a suggestion however; Joseph uses a story of a widow selling her wedding ring in a pawnshop, does that sound purely voluntary or free of manipulation or coercion?

Another side of this argument are the well meaning but frustrated activists that spout 'get money out of politics' or 'governments are corrupt- it's 'crony capitalism'. They're really fighting a losing battle. When lobbying is legal and government policy bought and sold in the interest of big business is inherent, we can begin to see how ridiculous and naive the request is. Democracy is bought and sold like anything/EVERYTHING else.

An elaboration/critique of the main point/s of the NLVs Argument

The core point that needs discussion with the NLV is on the fallacy of free trade as a guise for social control and dominance and on neo liberalism as the drive to hegemony. It essentially amounts to market discipline for the poor and social protection for the rich.

As we've discussed above everything is for sale, even (especially) government policy. If the power structure has any vested interest then it will corrupt, this is simply the gravitation. Economic philosopher Antonio Gramsci spent his life on this topic, which provide an exceptional illumination on this obscure gravitation; he popularised and expanded upon the concept of hegemony both cultural and economic. This is best summarised, I find, with a quote by the founder of the National Health Service in the UK, Aneurin Bevan *'How can wealth persuade poverty to use its political power to keep wealth in power? Here lies the whole art of Conservative politics in the twentieth century.'*

Once a political party that is in power is sufficiently in line with business interests then the goal of maximising profit can continue. The true free market, then, is really the freedom for big business to go unmolested into whatever ventures of accumulation, expansion and profit wherever, whenever in whatever manner they wish. The freedom they seek is the freedom to exploit labour unmolested and dump costs on the environment. The flaw of this whole argument, and where the NLV is directly hurting herself by saying it, is that the freedom they've just spouted usually means their exploitation and subjugation too. The connivance of the neo liberal apostles have managed to make the NLV conflate 'freedom' in this context to mean maybe freedom of speech, or freedom of press and will avidly defend the 'freedom' of markets to go a plundering unmolested. As articulated as 'cultural hegemony' by Gramsci.

Rule one of free market capitalism: free competition, utilise whatever means to gain advantage. It is an economy of oppression, the goal is to maximise profit, therefore you economise exploitation and oppression to achieve that. The liberty they spout as free trade is really a function of removing the liberty from someone else in their goal of seeking profit in the game of commerce. This root socioeconomic orientation results in brutal inequality both nationally and internationally.

The wests decadence is in direct correlation to the third worlds degradation[45]. The principal reason people in China, Brazil and South Africa type countries are seeing moderate improvements in quality of life is because their governments have managed to somehow wrangle a small amount of the global wealth and decrease the amount of exploitation currently being propagated on them. Countries like Sudan and Ethiopia still suffer brutal poverty.

We must understand that people aren't hungry through a lack of bread, only through a manmade economic function of where and how that bread gets produced and distributed. Their current corrupt governments compounded by neo-liberalistic policies of international free trade have put these people in brutal poverty in the first place. Immanuel Wallerstein has a good critique of this situation, in his view the core nations i.e. the traditional Western powers have created a system designed to extract wealth from peripheral nations and transfer it back into the core, in the past any attempt to change this system was met with military force, however as this became less of a viable option now it is economic warfare that is the weapon of choice, however the emergence of the BRICS seems to have upset the apple cart somewhat, but being realistic, China and the rest can exert greater economic power than ever before but they would be hard pressed to challenge the West, particularly the American military.

A quick example:
After the imposition of the International Monetary Funds (IMF) demands on 'opening the economy to free trade' as an incentive for a loan (with high interest rates) on India. The agriculture sector plummeted as Monsanto took over with GM mono crops. Farmers couldn't keep up and male farmers suicide rates soared as a result, figures in the hundreds of thousands[46]. For full details read the paper referenced, we don't have the scope to detail here but the point remains: corrupt developing nation governments are corrupt due to international financial institutions, controlled by the big bully on the playground. They proclaim: 'Come to our party, open up your economies to our interests or suffer the consequences'. Look what happened to basically all of South America. Dictators are placed in power if the democratically elected party steps out of line, ensuring a banana republic and western interests. The book *confessions of an economic hitman*' by John Perkins could be read to understand it in full, referenced prior. Essentially, These economic hitmen also operated in unison and still do with actual hitmen or death squads trained by the American military in the School of the Americas which can be linked to nearly every violent struggle in Latin America over the last 50-60 years, Nicaragua and Allende in Chile are prime examples[47].

Another perfect example of the fallacy in this argument is the fact that, according to a 2014 UN report, Africa loses more than it receives financially due to illicit financial flows[48]. A repeat of the counter argument in chapter 2 but the fact remains the same, only highlighting how devastating these illicit financial flows are on multiple levels.

Bottom line:
Freedom now only means the freedom of business to deal unabated on an international scope without foreign government hindrance. It's freedom for international corporations to exploit cheap labour and ever more resources. It's freedom for modern day rapacious free market capitalism to grow, as is required, to infinitum. It's the freedom to instil whatever neo-liberal globalised policies desired in foreign governments to allow this exploitation of labour and resource acquisition to continue unabated. It's freedom to control the population of said country. It's freedom to grow, exploit, grow, exploit and grow and exploit and dump costs onto the environment. Wage slavery is real, the freedom to choose between a Ford focus and a Vauxhall Mokka is not real freedom.

Below are some sample quick refutes you'd expect an NLV to use, again accompanied with quick sample responses.

HOW DID YOU READ JOHN PERKINS BOOK THEN? WE HAVE FREEDOM OF SPEECH AND THE PRESS

This is a bastion and must be protected at all costs. The freedom of speech and the press in the west really is exemplary but again, corporations have the 'freedom' to buy it up, change policy etc. to suit their needs. The result is now you see Rupert Murdock owning many 'news' papers and manufacturing consent to suit the established order. With which he and his buddies have been highly rewarded and maintain the status quo through the disinformation &/or misinformation to the masses.

But to quote Sociologist lecturer Jason Quinn in contradiction to this *'The Western lionisation of the concept of the Freedom of the press is problematic for me, underneath it all its not really free and never was. These Western ideals are open to serious question and for me are examples of the ingrained idea of Western exceptionalism that is used to justify the expansion of Western cultural hegemony. This goes hand in hand with the idea of liberal democracy being the only true form of government that can liberate the oppressed peoples of the world'*

Again, the conflation is the point that needs addressing. The ability for someone to speak out, write a book, an article and have a point of view is arguably the most important thing in the struggle to end oppression; Edward Snowden, Wikileaks, the banned book by Nicholas Shaxson all great examples. But its dangerous to also conflate that to mean Rupert Murdoch has the freedom to buy up all media companies if he wishes. Highlighting conflations to the NLV is key.

The book and documentary by Noam Chomsky and Edward S.Herman entitled manufacturing consent I think is the pertinent further reading/watching suggestion for the curious NLV[49].

PEOPLE HAVE FREEDOM TO CHOOSE WORK

People need to rent their bodies to an owner, which is open to coercion; it's essentially wage slavery.

The choice of work is limited by myriad factors, most notably peoples means and the level of unemployment hence ability of employers to hire, fire, put people against each other and dictate conditions.

Case in point is after the Black Death in England in the 14th century, it was known as the golden age of wages[50]. This was, unfortunately, due to a, in the most affected areas an 80% decrease in population from the disease. Resulting in the remaining workers having leverage, hence better wages. In normal circumstances wages are kept to a minimum in the pursuit of maximum profits through the exploitation of labour.

WE HAVE FREEDOM TO CHOOSE WHAT CHOCOLATE TO EAT

Freedom in product choice is highly nuanced, depending on myriad factors but none are free from coercion. Choice of goods consumption is submerged in coercion and manipulation through advertisement.
The advertisement industry is now huge, with the sole purpose of manufacturing wants and desires to suit whatever company pays them the best.

It has been studied, controversially, that with subliminal messaging your unconscious can 'make you want' a particular product[51]. If that particular product is bad for health, i.e. high sodium or sugar content and cause an increase in sickness across the population. Then we can rightly call it violent as it's directly linked to epidemiological negative effects.

Therefore even the ability to choose between 10 different types of chocolate is nice, the negative systemic outcomes aren't. As usual the NLV only takes an individualistic perspective though, no concern for the less able in society who are largely forced to consume unhealthy products, compounded by the fact that the level of choice described is really only open to 'some' privileged people at a scale of purchasing power.

15. IT'S MY PROPERTY, I OWN IT, I WORKED HARD FOR IT

Sample direct response

It's not the item itself you want or need, it's the utility the item gives you. Owning a Ferrari for example, it's only real use is for you to look cool? It's completely inefficient, there's no boot space to carry stuff, no room for passengers and you can't take it anywhere but the flattest roads. We need access to goods and services, not to OWN them.

Quick explanation of where the NLV is coming from

This statement speaks loudly of the NLVs indoctrination into the system that perpetuates the value disorder of modern day materialism and consumerism.

Property was created when we started to farm, then stuck up fences around those farms. This modern day knee jerk reaction to someone: *coming and stealing my stuff* is born out of the neo-liberal precursor of consumerism, which as described by Joseph *'reflects a sociological adaptation to the structural needs of our prevailing economic mode'*. In other words; the more people are coerced into purchasing property of their own, not sharing or reusing, the more product turnover there is, hence more profit.

The NLVs attitude is merely a sign of the level of historical brainwashing that has been accomplished on the masses. The attitude to suit the necessary function of unlimited capital accumulation is one of individualism compounded with a controlling attitude. Hence, the NLV acquires and puts up their fences, an individual measure of domination, flaunting of monetary wealth, posturing self-worth in a distorted value system.

Again, the growth of this sick mental disorder is not recent. Only exacerbated by the modern manifestation of domination, which we now call neo-liberalism. An attitude of self maximisation, domination, selfishness etc. was born out of the neo-lithic revolution, the current economic mode is still based on this archaic functioning and manifests today as greedy, hording, untrusting, selfish individuals. Again the root socio economic orientation is the fault, the preconditions produce the outcomes. In this context, irrational neurosis of hording materialism in the face of threats to survival/poverty.

These threats do exist but only because we have constructed a system of threats. Remove this precondition; hence the threats, then the individual should no longer act in that fashion. Pragmatically and simply (not easily) install a system of access to resources instead of private ownership of resources.

The core point here is: humans want to eat, drink, have the *craic* (*Irish word with no English translation*), play music, study philosophy and be comfortable and safe. These are all services or resources in one form or another. In a system of private property and domination, everyone is out to get everyone else's accumulated wealth.

Simply, and an abundance of explanation would be necessary on the pragmatics of a system of access but it the point is to merely imagine a system where access to these resources is maximised and no value is given to 'owning' an item. Please see Appendix A for a humble elaboration of this idea with examples.

An elaboration/critique of the main point/s of the NLVs Argument
This can be extrapolated to 2 major points:

First, to an individual who says he worked hard for his item and, second, to a business that claims intellectual rights.

Both are ridiculous, nothing is in isolation. Everything we 'own' is due to an amalgamation of every thought, ideal, innovation, creation of every human before you.

What makes this first point worse is the apparent signaling to others of how intelligent you are that you have acquired such property. Peter Joseph elaborates on this point expanding on how rich people flaunting extreme wealth *'is not a condition of sound mind and intelligence but a neurotic, disrespectable condition of immaturity and irresponsibility"*.

This demeaning behaviour further enforces and encourages the behaviour and attitude of 'MY PROPERTY' as it's basically about an exclusive club, in-group/out-group. People looking into the club feel more stressed and more social disorder occurs. Property ownership and the flaunting of it are basically detrimental to good relations between civilised humans in the 21st century. Joseph goes so far as to say *'the drive for material excess be seen for what it is- a sociologically driven mental illness"*.

Concurrently, and to delve into the second point on this: the item that some company makes e.g. apple and the iPhone. They don't *own* the intellectual property for this. The people that 'invented' that exact first 'iPhone' weren't just born with all the knowledge of humanity that gave them the base knowledge to manufacture it. In reality, a small part of it 'belongs' to the Egyptians, the Greeks, the Romans, Da Vinci, James Watt, Alan Turing etc. and those people owe their inventions and brilliance to the people before them. Patents and I.P rights are pure nonsense in a true sense, they only make sense within the logic of the markets game theory of commerce.

Society owes to society; nothing is in isolation. The surplus of capital is owed to everyone. As goods availability and quality grows so to should the standard of living for all in tandem. One person taking the profit for the combined work of humanity through history and through the current infrastructure (i.e. the schools that taught the workers and the hospitals that kept them healthy) is plainly just offensive in my opinion and a disgrace or a mockery to humanity.

Joseph again gives us a brief description of this which I feel accurately describes the idea: '*Access is at the heart of economic necessity, while ownership is a creation of the markets systems need to store value and property from theft in a world based on the assumption of universal scarcity. Most property crime is driven by want and a lack of access. The creation of an "access abundance", seeking to give everyone equal opportunity to use, means property crime would drop as abundance is achieved…people do not steal things they have access to*'.

Universal basic dividend as posed by Yanis Varoufakis[52] with the Diem25 team is a shining example. Essentially the spoils of capitalism, i.e. through the exploitation of humanity and the environment, could provide a dividend to the population. This could be used to pay for a Universal Basic Access[53], basically a means at which access to basic necessities is provided for everyone. We've been to the moon and seen back to the big bang, we can't provide food and water for everyone? Again, it's a market problem not a technical one. Market efficiency over technical efficiency.

With this practical step and a drive to move to an economy that supports access rights over property rights (maintaining some private property obviously for grannies pocket watch for example), one can imagine a level of sustainability and reduction of waste on an order of magnitude improvement.
In Appendix A, a further brief discussion is had on 'access'.

Below and slightly off topic but it can be expected at times in this argument by an NLV, a sample response given too.

I LIKE MY ROADS AND HOSPITALS, TAXES ARE ESSENTIAL

Is it ok to assume everything is going to plan when you give your money to some group of people in a room, that deliberate amongst each other, throw out some jargon, then don't build the social housing that's required but instead maintain nuclear weapons?

Would a more holistic, community scheme be better, where your community is self-sufficient and it's a community pot, with direct control by the community members. After that, but NOT before, a discussion can be had on what portion goes to regional, national, continental, international pursuits respectively? Only, again, agreed by an elected committee.

I don't have the answers obviously but the current tax system and the way tax is being spent is not working. A former Federal Reserve official, after quitting, described Quantitative Easing (QE) as just an ingenious way for tax money to go to the private finance sector, wall street[54].

This way of 'stimulating' the economy was in response to the loss of nearly 75% of global wealth (for lower classes: which literally meant their houses) after the financial sectors gambling habits blew up in their faces. The immediate solution was to bail out the banks with taxes, then spend taxes on QE while cutting down on money going to health & education etc. (Austerity). Insanity but not at all surprising in this system.

'This shit's got to go'

- Jacque Fresco

CHAPTER CONCLUSION

I think it important to not allow the NLV to erroneously jump to the conclusion that you don't advocate democracy. In contradiction an assurance that modern democracy is a triumph of the historical fight for liberty and equality and should be congratulated. However, the current form, controlled by capitalism and it's maturations of domination, is not functioning effectively. A reiteration to the NLV on the simple recognition there is still room for a lot of improvement. Just because one country is more democratic than another does not automatically mean it is a fully functioning democracy.

The old adage I think works nicely, supposedly said by Winston Churchill: democracy is the worst political system except for all the others. I believe the same could probably be said for capitalism, in regards to orthodox economic systems, not in its current financialised form and if we disregard negative effects to the environment.

What's abundantly apparent, globally, disregarding all the discussion here on the various particular points on the flaws of the current system of business freedom and business democracy is that it is completely out dated and insufficient to manage a global system of billions of people. The nation state idea within a global environmental system that does not care for those borders is obsolete. Perfect example is the ridiculous fan fare that is held in Westminster, England as MPs approach the bench holding a golden rod of some form, bow, take a step toward, bow again, take anther step etc.

Bottom line; contemporary democracy suffers a serious culture lag; we are stuck in Jurassic modes of social organisation while our level of technology proceeds in leaps and bounds. Archaic forms of government in the 21st century just do not have sufficient means to govern the myriad complexities of society in the 21st century, it is that simple. A complete overhaul of how governance is done must be incorporated. Hierarchies where one person is in control of millions of people is just not sound management, it is simply not possibly for a single human to function sufficiently on that scale. We need to use our level of technology- computers- to make those myriad decisions in a technical fashion, without bias and where debate is not applicable, in the same way you wouldn't debate the square root of 25 is 5. How that looks is a whole other topic, but one of extreme importance. See 'on genuine economics' in Chapter 5 for a brief opinion.

In the next chapter we will discuss a common rebuttal after we've sufficiently explained the flaws of our current economic mode and the resultant governance system. The ill informed NLV usually reverts to dealing in ultimatums in complete predictability to what we've just discussed in this chapter: *If you're against capitalism that means you must be a communist?* or *You must like to be controlled by a central authority, want everyone to be poor and the exact same!*

CHAPTER 4: YOU'RE A COMMUNIST

"We are all one. And if we don't know it, we will find out the hard way'
- Bayard Rustin

With the help of all the historical work of our predecessors in the pursuit to the end of oppression, I've tried to pose the argument for a new system in my day-to-day conversations. Immediately you'll be called a communist for proposing an alternative to capitalism. This ultimatum fallacy is discussed in the first argument below. Worse, during my myriad attempts to present ideas for a new economic system a common wall is encountered, met with abhorrent refusal. The reptilian fight or flight response kicks-in as they perceive you are attacking them personally, they've held those beliefs for so long.

Further, if you do fence off the reptile then you are met with a request to immediately spell out every nuance of how a better system would work.
Then when you make an attempt off the cuff, they pick holes, don't analyse the point nor look at the bigger picture. This will be discussed further in Argument #17.

I've come to the conclusion the majority of people find it extremely difficult to extrapolate one exemplary point into a systemic view. It's apparently extremely difficult for the human mind to calculate ramifications of indirectness. And extrapolate a macro perspective from an example, the synergies of the system don't compute if it is removed from them. An example is eating meat; the meat they eat is very far removed from the brutality of the slaughterhouses. Would people still eat so much meat if slaughterhouses were thrown in their face every time or the negative effects to the environment were more direct or obvious?

So, we are left with one option in this case, repeat the basics, win their hearts and hopefully they will be wise, smart, curious enough to research more egalitarian methods of society governance and genuine economic systems.

In the same breath, one must be diligent and make every attempt to guard their attacks. If at a loss and the NLV literally can't grasp the points a trick is to just bring it back to the base argument here *'we have no alternative than to have an alternative'* detailing the brutal level of poverty etc. As we've discussed before.

On another note, which I feel is quintessential to any argument for a new system: currently free market capitalism has no basis or attempt for large-order design, it's essentially the lazy mans route to economics, as stated abundantly before. So an appeal to the NLVs noble virtue of cooperative human ingenuity to triumph over adversity is quite a valuable argument.

An economic system, in the true sense of the word, requires hard work, cooperation, diligence, calculation and innovation, but the difficult things in life are the only ones worth doing. Appeal to this noble virtue perhaps. If anyone needs reminding of how amazing humans are, suggest they go see/listen to a live orchestra.

Below you will find a sample simple direct response to the argument, followed by a more detailed critique. Understanding a full concept is best achieved by the ability to explain it to yourself in metaphor. Therefore, during conversation with an NLV, we can find ourselves with the ability to bespoke the response, below are just samples I've personally come across. *'Capture their hearts and the mind will follow'*.

16. COMMUNISM KILLED 90 MILLION PEOPLE IN THE 20ᵀᴴ CENTURY

Sample direct response

First, That figure from the black book of communism has been considered inflated. But, the throes of contemporary capitalism are worse, killing 18 million every year through poverty according to one study. Neither of them work, we need something new altogether.

Quick explanation of where the NLV is coming from

Inevitably, The first argument you come against when you highlight an obvious modern failure like brutal poverty and that state bought free market capitalism is the core problem, you are usually struck with, by the NLV: *Well communism doesn't work, it killed 90 million people in the 20ᵗʰ century.* This is exemplary of the neo liberal gods indoctrination and commandment of anything outside its tenets as sacrilegious. You cannot raise a point on the flaws in contemporary capitalism without the immediate response *'communism is worse, you're a communist'.* An immediate challenge is pertinent in the vain of: *I didn't say anything about communism, we're talking about contemporary capitalism, the dominant economic system that holds sway, nearly global in scope'* (or at least it's tentacles are everywhere anyway).

The problem is the NLV immediately jumps to absolutes, nor any distinction given between actual communism and soviet and Maoist/Chinese communism. I'm not entirely sure why they do this but it does seem to be a culture of black and white politics, therefore black and white economics, hence black and white racial differences etc. It must be easier to control people if you have them in exactly 2 camps, divide and conquer. But 3 or more camps, possibly it can get out of hand and you lose some control? Again, oppression equilibrium must be maintained and the central effort of right wing politics is maintaining that persuasion of poverty to keep wealth in power.

Bottom line, we are not dealing in absolutes. I used the following statement before: 'only a sith deals in absolutes'; the joke worked in taking down their defences, luckily they were also a Star Wars fan. The point is that there are major structural flaws in contemporary capitalism, getting lost in absolutes and the statement *historical communism doesn't work either* is truncated, reductive and will get you no where.

Of all the people that I've had discussions with; some people raised in soviet communist nations and moved to more capitalist countries seem to be the most aggressive. They have an immediate position of something like: *how dare you say my country wasn't hard to grow up in, communism was brutal*. These people I find the hardest to reason with and the least open to conversation on the flaws of contemporary capitalism. Just because the grass is greener on one side doesn't make it a perfect field, there's serious problems in this field too. My opinion on this is don't bother; they see you as a spoiled capitalist child. Get the low hanging fruit first? People working on absolutes of capitalism and communism and can't get passed that will really struggle with the more abstract issues and complexities of the proposition of genuine economics (will be discussed in chapter 5).

These people along with people born and raised in opulence usually defend capitalism. They are, basically, either implicit or ignorant of where those luxuries come from, of which the minority enjoy extremely disproportionately. The fact the luxurious lives enjoyed by the minority is a function of supply chain slavery, oppression and exploitation seems to be lost on them. Ignorant or implicit doesn't change the core concept and the morally bad position of oppression remains. Whether it capitalism or communism the problem is a system of oppression, they both killed a lot of people. The NLV just needs reminding of that I feel.

An elaboration/critique of the main point/s of the NLVs Argument

The point on capitalisms throes of killing does still need elaboration in counterargument to this as the NLV will usually hold onto those numbers and repeatedly suggest *at least capitalism doesn't cause genocide.* Obvious examples of when it did cause genocide are the histories of Ireland and India-(Classical) liberal economics enforced by imperialistic Britain doomed millions to death and forced migration.

So the opposite is actually true of capitalism and there have been studies on the cause and effect of direct and indirect forms of violence, both structurally and behaviourally, as outgrowths of the maturations of the international capitalistic gaming logic which results in premature deaths, on a very large scale[55]. The number calculated by the Canadian peace research institute put the effect of poverty at 18 million people killed every year[56], and this was back in 1979, what are the numbers now? To quote professor of psychiatry James Gilligan on the effect of structural violence: *'Comparing this frequency of deaths from structural violence to the frequency of those caused by major military and political violence, such as World War II (an estimated 49 million military and civilian deaths, including those by genocide—or about eight million per year, 1939-1945), the Indonesian massacre of 1965-66 (perhaps 575,000) deaths), the Vietnam war (possibly two million, 1954-1973), and even a hypothetical nuclear exchange between the U.S. and the U.S.S.R. (232 million), it was clear that even war cannot begin to compare with structural violence, which continues year after year. In other words, every fifteen years, on the average, as many people die because of relative poverty as would be killed by the Nazi genocide of the Jews over a six-year period. This is, in effect, the equivalent of an ongoing, unending, in fact accelerating, thermonuclear war, or genocide, perpetrated on the weak and poor every year of every decade, throughout the world'*[57]

The points that need to be understood by the NLV, in fact everyone alive today, is that institutionalised violence or structural violence exists, it is deadly and it is the mother of behavioural violence. A child born in a third world ghetto, malnourished, dies of some disease (easily curable in the west) at the age of 5 is no different than another child being shot in the head (behavioural violence), in conceptual terms. The socio economic situation, through policies and man made ideologies (namely the gaming logic of markets) killed that child at 5. There is plenty of food and medicine available, technically. There is just a socioeconomic structure that prevented the child getting what it needed, not some natural phenomenon.

To quote Jason Quinn again in this context:
'A lot of social scientists argue that structural violence is a necessary condition for the birth of nation states, in conjunction with an external threat allegedly threatening the existence of the "mythical" homogenous people/nation that the nation state is beginning to coalesce around, one could argue very strongly here that the idea of the nation state is built upon an inherently violent and xenophobic foundation'.

When we have manmade systems that force people into poverty and desperation, the despicable behavioural violence we suffer today in society is only really to be expected as they fight for their very survival. On a macro scale we cannot account for the quantity of violence on an individual level, we have to take a systemic perspective, the socioeconomic system is the foundation of society, hence the precondition that produces this level of violence. With the quantity of deaths described through structural violence by the study and the level of behavioural violence experienced, from the constant creation of computer games of killing people to gangs and wars, we can concur *"socio-economic inequality can rightly be deemed the most destructive force on the planet"* through *'international trade dynamics that continue to isolate, deprive, and kill millions annually in the global south alone'*; as articulated by Joseph.

I don't feel we need to belabour the point. Further reading can be suggested, in particular the work of James Gilligan, where he draws on 25 years of work in the American prison system to describe the motivation and causes behind violent behavior. Nor is it helpful to get into a debate with an NLV on which system is worse; into a competition on how many people were massacred in genocides. The whole conversation is disgusting really. Converse on the positives instead and move onto the broader topic? Discussed in the next argument, #17.

Sample direct response
Depends on what you mean by 'works'?
Socialism in a particular country would function better than capitalism, in that it could most certainly reduce poverty. Or do you mean work as in more people would have yachts and Ferraris?

Quick explanation of where the NLV is coming from
The point the NLV raises here is usually one born out of a lack of knowledge, merely echoing the common rebuttal that's been incorporated in the anti-socialist rhetoric since day one. I would estimate that 90% of the people that use that argument about historical socialism would only have; maybe a general understanding of Stalin's regime, possibly the Khmer rouge and some recent news article about Venezuela, probably gotten from a private 'news' agency that has been bought out by Rupert Murdoch.

Within a proper debate on socialism vs capitalism the argument always centres on what works? Rarely do we find either side actually define what they mean by 'works' yet that is the core issue. The indoctrinated NLV has not, typically, analysed what they mean by works and spout that rhetoric merely as a contradiction to a brutal regime of communism. In doing so they inadvertently condone the brutalities of contemporary capitalism.

But what happens, again inadvertently, by the NLV is that we get stuck in a debate of double standards, where the NLV sits on a high horse position of privilege, being that they are within the capitalistic framework, dominant and controlling. From this point the NLV presumes, erroneously, that you are required to spell out a socialistic model in full, leaving no faults or flaws, to have any say in contradiction to contemporary capitalism. Further, this high horse privilege exempts them from any analysis of flaws in contemporary capitalism because, double standard wise, we're only talking about socialism.

A good approach here, I find, is to run a thought experiment with them. Ask them to pretend we are in a utopian society and the NLV is required to argue for a free market capitalist structure to society and allow you to argue against it. Very few NLVs will be able to describe contemporary capitalism in any meaningful way. I dare say no one could, the current economic mode is really chaotic, reactive, differs immensely by nation and frankly the whole thing is out of control. But if they do make a stab at it you can immediately begin to poke holes. Basically the NLV might try say things on innovation to which we have discussed before and you can pick holes immediately on producing poverty etc.

The point is that the NLV should see the cognitive dissonance/double standards and hopefully be more open to agree that capitalism is inherently flawed and we are not speaking about absolutes. Regardless of what economic system you call it; addressing flaws, creating poverty and environmental degradation, is what needs to be discussed. The discussion should be held on what *works*, in real terms.

Further points of clarity on the NLV's argument
The learned NLV will still have a point in that it's difficult to find a fully functioning socialist model, nation wide, functioning across sectors for an extended period of time. It's hard to argue the powerhouse current communist countries are really socialist in any core conceptual sense with how authoritarian the political systems are. But, I think it's fair to say, historically, no socialist experiment has ever been given the chance to flourish in full. It's always, without exception, been hindered on some scale by capitalist countries, with their inherent interest of dominance. Capitalism is

inherently a function of unequal domination, anything that threatens that domination & control must be crushed, as we've seen countless times in history and continue to see to this day.

A pertinent example is Spanish anarchism in the 1930s, which was working well, and probably the best example of a true attempt on equality across large sectors of society, but was faced with a war in the advent/midst of extreme fascism[58], not hard to see why that failed. War and fascism are like bread and butter; war and anarchism is an oxymoron. Worth noting here for congruence though: Soviet backed Spanish communists basically waged an internal war against the anarchist and socialist factions that were supposedly their allies against the fascists. The struggle of nation states in a global market bent on domination results in mayhem.

The emergence of the social democratic consensus within the more developed Western European nations in the aftermath of WW2 were designed to halt the spread of Soviet style communism. This saw the emergence of robust social welfare states in Germany, France, the UK and others as well as increased labour rights, unionisation, socialised healthcare, free education, nationalised industries etc. however it also created the conditions necessary for the emergence of neoliberalism.

For more examples a list can be found on Wikipedia under 'list of anarchist communities'

Of note:

- Zapatistas, Chiapas, Mexico
- Left wing Kurdish Movement, Rojava, Syria
- Hungarian rev 1956

Succinctly, Communism and socialism, what they really represent in their origins, or their idealised structure to society, is an attempt to remove hierarchal systems of control where monetary wealth gets concentrated at the top. They also, however, corrupted because of the core ethos of perceived rigid and universal scarcity, compounded by the need to trade internationally and the hegemony of the countries that espouse free trade (of course they do as they are the ones rewarded by it). Unfortunately, Free enterprise got there first and set the rules of the house. Now those rules are adamantly, viciously and aggressively instilled, policed, and maintained.

But the key to this argument, in my opinion, is to not get stuck in labels; neither capitalism nor socialism is or has 'worked' in any form because we are still suffering brutal inequality, poverty, violence and environmental degradation. The question is on what works and what doesn't. The metric of what we mean by 'works' needs to be exactly that, the focus of removing inequality, poverty and maintaining a sustainable environmental system. What label you wish to put on that is irrelevant. The only thing that is relevant is the means at which we achieve that, in a technical fashion.

Resources are all that matters, and access to them, to eat, drink and breathe, to educate, health and happiness. Call it socialism if you will, all it really is; is anything that doesn't have one human as the owner or controller of another and earths natural resources are common heritage for everyone. An economic system that at it's core is designed, in a technical fashion, without ideology or subjectivity to algorithmically calculate the requirements for liberty from poverty and maintaining sustainability is all that matters.

From here we can bring the NLV to begin to speak about genuine economics. Which the arguments against any new system will be discussed more in chapter 5, including further discussion on a purposed genuine economic system and suggested steps of transition. Maximising already incorporated parts of the 'sharing' economy for example.

Below a further argument expected with a quick sample response.

LOOK AT VENEZUELA NOW? AND CUBA NEVER WORKED?

Complex issues, complex different countries, different cultures, different histories, different resources etc.

We can't jump to the conclusion: socialism doesn't work, because of some metric you've conjured up, or the IMF has conjured up and concurs it doesn't *work*.

Cuba has one of the highest literacy rates, lowest infant mortality rate, amongst other metrics in Latin America, and has a similar life expectancy with the US[59]. I would agree it doesn't *work* on a metric of freedom of press, for example, but again we don't jump to the conclusion on the left that Cuba *works* fully/completely because we have some metrics of functionality. Systemic structuralist perspective again must be taken to take a full view.

Venezuela has what's now being said the largest quantity of oil in the world. Prior to the socialist revolution it was fully open for international free trade, the people remained in poverty regardless. They have suffered economic sanctions, propaganda and all the rest of the tactics deployed to subvert their government ever since, all in the interests of global *free* trade hegemony of control and *freedom* (business freedom to acquire profit unmolested). Again under real metrics, Venezuela was doing great in advancing social housing, reducing poverty and increasing education[60], but that doesn't matter does it? Their GDP is not maximising profits for the elite, therefore: *Socialism doesn't work.*

A truncated, simplistic, reductive view full of double standards!

We are at loggerheads with most people caught in the framework of the neo-liberal dogma. A version of absolutism has become sacrosanct, where if you critique capitalism you must be a communist. The brutal communism under Stalin then an umbrella term used to disparage any system outside of the neo liberal gods church. Regardless of what logic you purpose; stating it's not communism nor a utopia, one is ultimately confronted with this truncated logic: *Communism didn't work so anything outside capitalism will not work, it's just too hard to make changes, let's just keep it the way it is.*

To simply say something cannot be done because it seems too difficult is absolute stagnation, the only reason this stagnation is accepted is due to the interests of the already powerful, they will not concede to a new system when the current system has rewarded them so generously, hence you get the general apathy of any change through the masses by the means of a manufactured consent, again a form of social control. Social control by the ruling elite should not be confused for human laziness or unwillingness to seek change for the better, to solve problems with our ingenuity. To allow this control allows the lobotomising of the group mind. The elimination of poverty can and most certainly should be done, at least tried, with an economic system that is focused at its core on that endeavour, not just as a 'trickle down' effect.

This is the core tenet of a genuine economic system, structurally focused to remove poverty within environmental limits. However, we will immediately run into another form of fight or flight, the reptile will re-emerge from the depths of the thalamus and claim adamantly *that will never happen* or *you're living in a utopian fantasy* or the most depressing argument from an NLV; *what will people do if we don't have to work so much?*

We'll all suffer forever because it's *TOO HARD to* change and even if we do, people will have nothing to do without a *job* so lets not bother. It's depressing and depletes confidence in our species but persevere, we're actually really close to at least having them open minded to a genuine conversation…in chapter 5 we'll have a look at why and at some of the knee jerk defensive reactions one would expect.

CHAPTER 5: CHANGE CAN NEVER HAPPEN

"If you think we can't change the world, it just means you're not one of those who will."

- Jacque Fresco

"You never change things by fighting the existing reality. To change something, build a new model that makes the existing model obsolete."

- R. Buckminster Fuller

"From a systems-based scientific perspective, what is proposed here is simply what a real economy is, by definition"

- Peter Joseph

Joseph quotes this after a very detailed account of the flaws of the current system with transition suggestions into a more sane system. The 5 key points posed in his book are abundantly logical and after analysis of appendix B, where he goes into detail on genuine economic calculation, one can see the logic. The book is called the 'The *new human rights movement*'

Currently the economic system is based on a perceived level of scarcity of resources. Foundationally to free market capitalism is the accepted fact that there is an insufficient amount of resources and that's entirely what the planet provides. Regardless of what we do there's not enough to go around, this idea is considered fact and unquestionable. Therefore a system of competition is needed to allocate what little life supporting resources we have to the most deserving. When this is adherently agreed upon with no question, competition ensues to secure your share, hence your survival, of the scarce resources. This is compounded by a bastardisation of Darwin's tenet of 'survival of the fittest', it has been twisted to mean 'strongest' or 'most dominant' when really it means most able to adapt to ones environment.

Naturally this fight for bread produces winners and losers as a mathematical certainty. This result of winners and losers is called inequality. This level of inequality experienced produces poverty. Poverty has been shown to be a main driver for a vast array of negative outcomes suffered by humanity today. From xenophobia to racism, behavioural violence to high infant-mortality rates, prostitution to paedophilia, gangs to war[61]. However, these negative outcomes are then simply blamed on nature because there simply wasn't enough to go around, so it's *just the way things are*.

Granted, we are not all equal and we all have different strengths, but this system demands the inherently weak to strive to be the strongest, when it's physically, pragmatically and mathematically not possible for everyone to succeed in the game of commerce. The punishment for this failure is poverty, a street and premature death. This is simply barbaric, shameful and negligent. A system that instead shames the inherently strongest for not feeling proud to support fellow human beings that were born less fortunate than her, seems to me the obvious path to dignity, respect and integrity.

The book *the spirit level* by Professors Richard Wilkinson & Kate Pickett give empirical evidence of the negative effects of inequality in great detail, referenced above. Yet further, the effects of *feeling* poor also have huge ramifications on society, the humiliation of feeling less than someone else, natural in an unequal society, causes huge stress and negative psychosis, as described in the next book on this topic by the same authors, titled: *The inner level*[62]. Stress has been proven to be a precondition in most heart disease, currently the biggest killer suffered today. Literally, inequality is killing us[63]; there is an abundance of work on this topic in support of this[64].

Essentially, The current socio-economic system forces and creates poverty, artificial poverty; the biggest killer there is or ever has been. Crazily and in stark contrast to the required level of scarcity: the system also requires infinite growth, growth through the consumption of resources, on a finite planet! The systems mechanical requirements have permeated into the psychology of the people and instilled a level of constant dissatisfaction, so that you will forever seek to be satisfied through the acquisition of goods (resources). This constant growth, through dissatisfaction, over shoots the planets capacity to recuperate[65].
We call it consumerism and it is complete negligence, immature and irresponsible.

Ergo, We **NEED** an alternative, we no longer have the luxury to discuss whether it's required or not, whether the quantity of Ferraris manufactured will be sufficient for the affluent or not. Whether the flawed attempts of the past to emancipate the working class were flawed or not? A step away from the barbarism we now live in is **NEEDED**, not desired. Poverty is rampant, inequality brutal, homelessness epidemic, disease, war and won't someone please think of the children? *There is no alternative but to have an alternative system.*

Essentially, we have no choice but to make a step toward an alternative system that recognises the flaws and makes a step in a progressive fashion from those flaws. Understanding the flaws, the ideology behind them and helping to illuminate this to everybody affected by it is the first step in that progressive line. To which I humbly wish to support.

To that end, below are some simple responses to some common expected arguments on how any other system in contradiction to the neo-liberal gods church won't work, it's utopian and you're living in a fantasy world.
A sample simple direct response is given to the argument, followed by a more detailed critique of the problem and finally a discussion on a genuine economic system.

Understanding a full concept is best achieved by the ability to explain it to yourself in metaphor. Therefore, during conversation with an NLV, we can find ourselves with the ability to bespoke the response, below are just samples I've personally come across.
'Capture their hearts and the mind will follow'.

18. WE CAN'T MAKE ANY CHANGE; TOO MANY PEOPLE WOULD SUFFER, WE RELY TOO HEAVILY ON THE CURRENT MARKET SYSTEM AND HYDROCARBONS

Sample direct response
In a word: yes, but it would be an ever decreasing reliance, Instead of an ever increasing reliance in the current system.

Quick explanation of where the NLV is coming from
This argument by the NLV shows a good understanding of how entrenched we are within the current system and it's power structures. Any alleviation from one thing has knock on effects when we are embedded in a system of exploitation and individual profit. An example being the rise in veganism, the alleviation of brutal oppression of animals has the knock on effect of an immediate loss of revenue in the meat industry supply chain.

The main point here is the recognition that the market system is at fault, not the nodes in the supply chain network. Using the veganism example again, the need to stop cutting forests down for livestock farms greatly outweighs the temporary loss of revenue in the meat industry supply chain. Animals are suffering brutal conditions and dying in millions for the momentary pleasure of our palates, this compounded by the devastating mal effect to the environment. The market system needs to adapt, farmers need to adapt their practices to meet a plant based diet demands. The core point is; just because there will be revenue loss in the meat industry does not warrant a justification to continue the brutal and environmentally devastating practise of livestock raring. The point is that the market is at fault, in that individual profit is all that matters; removing instruments of exchange (regardless if they are inhumane or devastating to the environment) is completely disregarded. The profit motive is sacrosanct and the law on the protection of private property is all that matters, as we've discussed in chapter 3.

So to conclude in quick counter argument with the NLV: the market system is the flaw producing these problems. We cannot continue to allow suffering and environmental degradation because making changes to the market will result in market inefficiencies. This is frankly absurd, the adjustments aren't desired but they are necessary, the temporary negative effects are also unavoidable. Ensuring adjustments are made in a concerted, planned, systemic, organised, periodical fashion to mitigate as much as possible the mal effects is completely feasible.

Allowing the market to continue on a business a usual (BAU) path, with no effort to incorporate adjustments of mitigation will result in vastly more devastating outcomes in the near future. Again, the reference provided in chapter 2, argument #8 on biodiversity loss by the convention on biological diversity is a pertinent example but only one of many. The various BAU scenarios envisaged by institutions studying these phenomena all look scarily bleak[66]. If further justification is required, one needs only look out the window, we are already suffering major problems in poverty, violence and environmental loss.
Not having a plan to mitigate the devastating effects inevitably coming is absurd, negligent and cowardly. Remind them of that.

An elaboration/critique of the main point/s of the NLVs Argument
The core counter argument here and the one that needs expansion is:
We need to accept where we are now as a species. We've majorly messed up and we need to hold our hands up and say: Yes, We've

messed up. Without that acceptance there is no argument to make changes. With that acceptance we can agree to make changes that incorporate mitigation. This mitigation is where we can expound the conversation in showing the vast potential of poverty and environmental degradation alleviation with the correct application of technology.

A perfect example would be the use of hydrocarbons, not in the further production of BAU, but in the use in an ever-decreasing fashion toward a fully renewable energy system. It is correct, more hydrocarbon burning will result in further heating of the atmosphere, but if we accept that that is inevitable due to our current mess up then we can use what's in the ground as a means of mitigating against a BAU and incorporating a zero CO^2 energy economy. We have no choice but to accept the people working in that industry will suffer losses in revenue (which means the ability to pay bills for most of the exploited in the supply chain) but all we can do is accept that and mitigate the ramifications as best we can. Allowing it to continue in BAU is simply and quite frankly not an option.

Once this core point has been accepted by the NLV (if ever) then a discussion is advised on post scarcity potentials. This really highlights the lack of need to be stuck in a market ideology that hinders technological application in the interest of profit motives.

In appendix A of *The new human rights movement* entitled '*Post scarcity potentials*', Joseph goes into an abundance of detail on what can be achieved in a hypothetical scenario of full technological application. It is an extrapolation to highlight potentials and provides the logical argument that there is a cultural lag behind technological application, but with potential applications the argument on scarcity of food, water and energy becomes essentially mute. For the benefit of this text I'll briefly give an overview, highlighting the key points.

'Many in technology communities today do talk about positive future possibilities; with the implication being "we are just not there yet". The truth is that currently existing methods, not trending potentials, can already solve the food, water, energy, pollution, and basic material stress problems common today, if scaled out properly in a systems based approach.' With regards Food: *'if we extrapolate the theoretical potential of this method and all agricultural land on Earth was modified to only use vertical farming methods, the output would be enough to feed 34.4 trillion people'* however *'only 0.03 percept of that potential is needed. This makes moot any seemingly practical objections to this extrapolation.'* With regards Water: *'According to ultraviolet water purification statistics produced by a facility in New York, only 3,324 facilities would theoretically be needed to purify all the water currently used* (globally), *requiring only 12,309 acres of land.'*

Joseph then goes into great detail about various potentials of renewable non-hydrocarbon energies such as solar, wind, geothermal and hydropower. The concept remains the same that the potential vastly outweighs what's required in a theoretical fashion and the figures and calculations given confirm this. Joseph does however conclude by stating *'the key to a sustainable energy abundance comes down to an integrated systems approach combining base load and more localised mixed-use/reuse systems…while critics of renewables cite the native limitations, such as the intermittency of wind farms or solar energy, the key rests in the combination of these means, along with intelligent localised sources, such as domiciles with heat pumps, small wind turbines and so on.'*

If the NLV states, which she probably will: *'it's way more complex than just building 3,324 facilities'*, then a reply in the affirmative with a definition of 'theoretical extrapolation' and a confirmation on the core argument that contemporary capitalism is only interested in short term profits and any alleviation of energy scarcity for example is just an after thought or side effect.

Below is an expected reply from the NLV in this conversation.

WHAT ABOUT ALL THOSE JOBS THAT WOULD BE LOST

Again, Jobs is not what people need, people need access to resources. The transition would only remove a job (access to resources) when the automated accessible updated version is accessible, combine this with a Universal Basic Access (UBA) to basic resources then the argument is mute.

For example, in free market capitalism you couldn't (if possible) just cure cancer tomorrow, it's a nearly-150 billion USD industry[67] made up of treating the problem, curing it would put millions of people out of work. It would have to be slowly devolved, BUT again, it most certainly should be.

In the next argument, #19, more discussion on what 'jobs' are in this context.

19. IF MACHINES DO EVERYTHING, WHAT WILL PEOPLE DO? PEOPLE NEED JOBS

Sample direct response

First, do you think people like waking up at dawn, commuting to work for an hour in packed trains and working 8 hours a day, doing the same monotonous arduous labour day in day out? Most jobs are degrading, poorly paid and backbreaking.

People need security, food, health, community and a meaningful vocation in life; please don't confuse that with 'jobs'!

Quick discussion on this, as we've discussed it before

We briefly discussed this in argument #'s 4 & 5 were we posed the counterarguments that people are perceived lazy as a result of difficult meaningless work and that the bastardisation of the word *job* is largely conflated. This conflation argument by the NLV is usually presented as a defence for *the 'honest workingman'* maxim but, depressingly, suggests that without some form of arduous coerced labour role, the honest workingman would simply laze on his couch all day and die shortly after of boredom. How this argument is even entertained, and entertained it is by vast quantities of people, is really astounding to me. Nothing could be more logical or blatantly obvious, without the need for justification that people would not succumb to a sedentary life if not coerced to do so.

Obviously there would be a small percentage of people that would just do nothing but I feel the contrary numbers to the current numbers would be the case in reality. We currently have a percentage of people overweight and lazy which seems logically to stem from a lack of agency in life, as discussed in chapter 2. In a hypothetical system free from that coercion and exploitation with freedom to pursuit whatever you see fit; the percentage of people sedentary would vastly decrease. In my opinion, this is one of the arguments with an NLV that you can really just laugh off at how preposterous it is. There is an encouragingly high quantity of very active people, even within the current 60 hour total work week paradigm, that use their free time in a variety of helpful and productive ways. One pertinent example: 'Doctors without borders', where highly skilled doctors travel to help the most needy, in dangerous places very far from home for a fraction of the salary they would expect as private doctors.

Concurrently, society as a whole is guilty of this bastardisation too where even trade unions will fight for 'jobs', sometimes even at the detriment of technological progression. This contradiction is exemplary of the obvious fact, as has been discussed in chapter 2, that technological advancement is the means at which to remove arduous labour hence providing better working conditions for the working class. Which, correct me if I'm wrong, is the core ethos & struggle of trade unions. This goal of focusing technology on decreasing arduous meaningless employment should be the goal.

The counter argument should be presented first in the correct context of jobs. 'Jobs' are social constructs to coerce ones labour, the threat of poverty; the compulsion to work and the money received; the contract with which you submit. To quote Joseph: *'"jobs" are not vocations. Jobs are structural prerequisites for survival in an economic system based upon labour for income'*.

When we have successfully gotten this point across to the NLV and the point that these social constructs for relief from the threat of poverty are first and foremost a function of exploitation to maximise profit for the capitalist owner. That this is done through the inherent goal of minimal working conditions, maximum hours and the least benefits, which manifests as arduous, backbreaking, rat race, underpaid labour. Then the advance of technology, in the context of removing jobs through the application of automation, is a core fundamental flaw or crux to the system. Finally then the argument can be made that the goal of a civilised society should be to, logically, remove these structural prerequisites that hinder technological progress and cause human suffering.

In a sentence: technological unemployment should be the goal, not the problem.
More discussion on how to achieve an automated society without allowing people to succumb to the neo liberal gods threats of poverty are explored in Appendix A under notes on themes-theme 1 Automation.

A slightly off topic argument, but could be presented, is given below with a sample response.

WHAT ABOUT WORK THAT HAS NO CONSTRUCTIVE VALUE?

Like a monk praying or a painting? Or like a multi billion dollar industry of people looking at candlesticks on screens and guessing on what way they will rise or fall and monetarily profiting from it; not constructing or contributing to anything in any tangible or practical sense (essentially parasites). Or how advertisements are literally in the business of brainwashing you into purchasing their specific product. No part of the advertisement is informative, if it was a car manufacturer advert would simply have the specs of the car detailed and how it compares to previous or other models.

But that aside, there is a discussion to be had that one needs to have a system that can give value to something that has no real constructive use. Like a painting, how does one value a painting without money?

Again, this is a value disorder where we have been raised into considering an item (especially of art or music) only can be valued on monetary scale.

In a sane system, where social nets are abundant; the choice of people to paint pictures for their lives is available to everyone and the merits at which it is accepted is the same as in the current system (except the monetary goal of course); social recognition, praise from your peers, and satisfaction in achieving artistic tasks. The value then is exactly what the community of painters say it is. A purposed question then I think helps: if you had 10 professional artistic painters and 100 new pieces of painted art by various artists, would every artist be able to precisely value the painting in monetary terms without knowing which artist did the painting? I think not, the monetary value is arbitrary and fully dependent on social conventions on trade, commerce, reputation and so on.

The point is: free market capitalism is no better at valuing the worth of some artists painting than any other hypothetical system without a monetary value system, in fact I'd go further to suggest it thwarts artistic value where you find paintings that are worth 20 million dollars for no other reason than someone said so. What matters is: whatever society values the piece of art in real terms is it's value through peer recognition and one can never predict that.

20. THAT'S A UTOPIAN IDEAL; YOU'RE CRAZY, THAT CAN NEVER HAPPEN

Sample direct response

This is not a utopia, it's not perfect, and nothing is. It's not about my opinion or yours. It's about what works and what doesn't work. The question is a technical one not a moral one, and this just makes far more logical sense than the devastating game of contemporary capitalism.

Quick explanation of where the NLV is coming from

This argument from the NLV is really the final hurdle. They've taken in everything and accepted the logic but for some reason a final ditch effort from the reptilian brain lashes out, it's the fear that acceptance will suddenly change everything in their lives and change is *scary*. It usually follows after statements like *'that makes logical sense but...'* or *'I can see how that would solve that problem but...'*

The fear of change seems here to be the main problem and the ingrained belief that anything outside the neo-liberal gods commandments is just fanciful stuff of fiction. This is an exemplary point of how truly pervasive the neo-liberal god has become, the level of indoctrination where if someone poses an improvement to a serious problem that is causing deep suffering, you are met with a defence that you must be living in a fairy world. Again, brutal poverty is essentially a God given part of nature and anything outside that must be a 'utopia' and you must be crazy in trying to resolve or even alleviate it.

Essentially, They use the utopian term to make you sound like an illogical/irrational dreamer or that you are suffering from delusions of fantasy. It's important to immediately dispel this by stating clearly, 'this is not a utopia, it's not perfect', even using the word utopia yourself in conversation at any point seems to illicit a response, so best to avoid it in my opinion. It's about what works and what doesn't: technical efficiency instead of arbitrary market efficiency.

An elaboration/critique of the main point/s of the NLVs Argument

As we've said the NLV has seen the logic but is afraid of change. The structures to free market capitalism and how a genuine economic system would look need to be elaborated on to present the fundamental technical question of genuine economics in contrast to the market question of economising monetary profits. This seems a viable way to critique their point and frames the discussion.

Framing in a step by step way:
Scarcity is the curse, yet scarcity is the rule. All interactions in market economics are based on the 'fact' that resources are scarce, there's not enough to go around and all resources are rigidly universally scarce. Competition the driver then to acquire your share. This was most notably put forward by Thomas Malthus in the early 19th century and the resulting die offs, when inevitably, some people don't get their fair share was dubbed the 'Malthusian trap'.

The Malthusian traps assumption on reality is that food supply cannot be controlled and it is <u>static,</u> hence; when the population increases above a certain threshold, food supply stays the same and people die off. The core of contemporary market ideology finds its basis on this and expands its assumptions in that; as population increases the raw <u>resources required </u>(wheat, water, iron, oil etc.) to support them also stays the same. Ergo, if a population doubles, resource quantities must also double to support them. As can be seen with the modern assumption that resource overshoot is the result of over-population.

In reality however, as the population increases the quantity of resources required to support them is not static nor is it linked to population growth. Resource quantities are fully dependent on the application of technology. The quantity of resources required to support a given population can be decreased with an increase in efficiency (productive means, extraction techniques, processing, distribution, recycling etc.) and an increase in efficiency-in-use (doing more and more with less and less/ephemeralisation). Ergo, if a population doubles, there is no link on how much food can be produced to feed the population. There's nothing to say that food supply couldn't increase ten fold with the respective required application of technology to accomplish that level of efficiency.

Exemplary of this is when Norman Borlaug discovered how to vastly increase the yield of wheat[68]. He has been given the title of 'the saviour of billions' but let's be clear; he did not change 'nature', he, and the team of scientists, applied technology to solve a problem, they applied a technical solution and increased abundance of a food supply, therefore providing for more people and increasing the standard of living. This was through human ingenuity to increase efficiency, not some uncharacteristic generosity of the neo-liberal god. Further, it was the some of agricultural science, not just his ingenuity.

Therefore, in contradiction to the Malthusian traps assumption on reality; scarcity is neither static nor universal. One resource and/or another can be increased with technical efficiency; hence the trap does not exist. Market ideology does not find its basis in reality, only in assumptions. Static, scarce and insufficient quantity of resources only exists in the minds of orthodox economists; resource-overshoot as a result of over-population only exists in the ideology of markets. The problem with this ideology is that the ramifications are deadly; as negative effects (Resource-overshoot, brutal poverty, devastating global health problems, pan-environmental degradation, bio-diversity loss) are seen as an outgrowth of nature, 'just the way it is' and nothing got to do with flaws in manmade systems/institutions (markets, neo-liberal economic ideology, the IMF etc.)

Nothing could be further from the truth; these negative effects are completely manmade through market ideology, now in its modern manifestation of globalised financial capitalism driven by neo-liberal economic ideology. A true or genuine economic system would/should focus on maximising efficiency (methods as above), hence maximising the quantity of life support resources availability, ergo minimising scarcity, hence poverty. Minimising scarcity of resources, maximising abundance of life support resources, within environmental limits is the definition of a genuine economic system. This again is just a technical equation of applying the best available technology at the time. The Best Available Technology Not Exceeding Environmental Limits (BATNEEL). A genuine economic system is a quest in the understanding of what the level of scarcity truly is overall, across the whole planet for everyone and how to overcome it on all relevant levels, ending socioeconomic inequality, hence poverty.

It's not subjective progressive left wing policy, heartening community spirit nor a lovely song claiming one love; it's about calculating resource quantities, consumption rates, replenishment rates then applying the best available technology to maximise efficiency in the abundance of life support resources therefore minimising scarcity, inequality and poverty through best design, production, distribution and recycling methods, all within environmental limits.

In the same way the square root of 25 is 5; the equation for maximising resource abundance is not up for debate, it's a technical equation. In '*The new human rights movement*', Joseph details it in full; everyone needs to understand this if we are to solve the myriad problems facing our species in the 21st century.
My suggestion then: read the book, write a summary in 2-4k words and give that to someone else (the NLV you've just won over?) with the same suggestion (#understandpoverty).

Bottom line, we need to show how it <u>can</u> happen, we can control the selfish gene for our mutual benefit, the majority of people don't have to live a life of poverty, we can meet environmental limits and live sustainably on this planet. We can have a truly genuine economic system, I do hope I live to see that realised and see then what societies assumptions are on 'human nature'.

What we hopefully have now arrived at with the NLV is a question to pose to *them*: Are we in conclusion that whatever you want to call the current economic system: be it free market capitalism, a global corporate hegemony aristocracy, state communistic global dictatorships or whatever it is, it is simply not functioning correctly, and devastatingly so? hence the question is not whether we *should* make fundamental changes to economical systems but *how?*

I most certainly don't have all the answers but I can relay a very logical alternative brought forward, initially, by the great works of R.Buckminster Fuller and Jacque Fresco. Jacque Fresco called it a resource based economy and devoted his life to practicalities of how cities etc. could/would look, his work continues on with the research group, the Venus Project[69]. Buckys research continues with the Buckminster Fuller institute[70]. Peter Joseph and the non-profit 501(c) sustainability advocacy group called the zeitgeist movement then further articulated this, with the knowledge of current technologies, and elaborated on the concept. This is sometimes now refereed to as a Natural Law Resource Based Economy (NLRBE). Again, the title doesn't matter, call it whatever you like. The core concept has and will always be the same, it is just a genuine economic system, as described.

I have tried to simplify some areas of transition posed below with further discussion in Appendix A under notes on themes but a full understanding can only be reached by reading the book '*The new human rights movement*' and/or watching the lecture presented by Peter Joseph which can be viewed on YouTube under the title '*economic calculation in an NLRBE*'. He also now has a very well articulated podcast called 'Revolution Now!' for those that prefer to listen.

SO WHAT IS A LOGICAL ALTERNATIVE, WHAT DO WE MEAN BY GENUINE ECONOMIC MODEL?

Firstly; a brief definition from Joseph:

'Unlike the market, which is structurally based on scarcity, trade, competition, and exploitation, this new model focuses on strategic and sustainable abundance, collaboration and balance' It *'is about constructing an economic system technically and objectively....the logic is no different in principle from the practical decision to reject using a manual screwdriver in favour of an electric one, increasing productive efficiency'*. If an 'ism' is required then *'the perspective is structuralist'* in that *'structuralism simply means we are accounting for larger order relationships when thinking about social affairs'*.

It encompasses 5 'shifts', presented simply as a suggested meaningful way to begin transition away from the competitive market of oppression, exploitation and poverty; or a practical application to reduce scarcity pressure and increase economic efficiency (in a practical sense) to relieve poverty and destruction of the environment:

- Maximise automation
  - Alleviate human labour
  - Provide universal basic access & a dividend to supplement people out of 'jobs' as automation increases
  - Most arduous jobs are first to be automated
  - Can work to really bring about the 'green new deal' idea
- Promote an access economy- Shared commons
  - Producer is the owner of the full life cycle of goods,
    - Maximises incentive to recycle and removes inherent and planned obsolescence

- o Universal standardisation of good components across as many sectors as possible
    - Minimises wasteful practices & maximises recycling potential
- Open source- Participatory economics- collaborative commons
    - o Away from IPs and toward collaboration, maximising innovation
- Localisation instead of globalisation
    - o Maximise production/distribution efficiency- reduce waste, minimise transport, ease of recycling
- Digital network feedback
    - o Using the internet of Things (IOT) as a basis to manage resources in real time

Again, I discuss these a bit further in Appendix A but this has been articulated in far greater detail in chapter 5 of '*The new human rights movement*'. But what's important here to note is that none of these 5 shifts illustrated are novel ideas, they are all currently happening already in one or way or another within the current system, the point is to focus our whole economy on maximising their potential:

- Automation is ratcheting-up as we speak.
- The sharing economy- bike share, uber, timebanks, AirBnB etc. - are on the rise steadily*.
- The open sourcing of platforms and ideas is now on a significant scale across all sectors- Wikipedia, Linux, Tesla releasing car designs etc.
- The 'local grown' drive is coming in leaps and bounds; from farmers markets, fair trade, local grown produce and people getting 'off the grid'

- Finally the Internet of Things showing how we are more digitally connected to everything every day.

* NB: The sharing or gig economy while a good idea in principle has been corrupted and used to exploit the precariat, it's a double edged sword. The idea is great but there are obvious problems with it, which is unsurprising in our current economic mode of inherent and incentivised dominance, manipulation, advantage seeking and exploitation.

From there and assuming transition along this path is smooth with minimum negative push back (which is extremely unlikely with how well the system has rewarded the people in power now) then a good conversation can be had on what a true/genuine economic system would operate like. The core concept is really a simple (but not easy) technical equation of maximising efficiency in design, production, distribution and recycling. I won't go into detail here as I don't feel I could do it justice and as it's described in abundant detail of Appendix B of '*The new human rights movement*' and in the lecture presented by Peter Joseph which can be viewed on YouTube under the title '*economic calculation in an NLRBE*'.

But let me give you this simple sample 'equation' Joseph presents, which I hope will spark your interest and inspire you to more research on the purposed model of genuine technical economic system processes:

$$f_p(E_{design}, E_p, E_{dist}, E_r) \rightarrow max$$

Where:

- $f_p =$ Production function
- $E_{design} =$ Design Efficiency

- $E_p =$ Production efficiency
- $E_{dist} =$ Distribution efficiency
- $E_r =$ Recycling efficiency
- $\sim> max =$ simply the goal of maximising the efficiency of all

Joseph goes into a lot more detail of the nuances of this of course. But important to note, and in closing, in Josephs words *'the purpose of this…is to give an overview of optimized economic calculations on the core, technical level, highlighting the most relevant, overarching needs or attributes. A more detailed and complete algorithmic calculation, taking into account all sub processes in real-life terms, along with democratic participation (participatory economics), would require a great deal more expansion'.*

That algorithm, participation and expansion he speaks of encompasses nothing less than, arguably, the most important endeavour the human species in the 21st century could undertake, if not in its total existence to this date. I plan to play a part in that discussion, action and realisation; do you?

TO CONCLUDE IN SUMMARY

With an understanding of:

- The core flaw in classic/orthodox economic market ideology and it's devastating ramifications to global human & environmental health,
- A conceptual arrangement on the technical equation of genuine economics- maximising efficiency in a real sense- to

alleviate poverty through the core intention of minimising scarcity
- The potentials of the technologies we currently have available to us (described in argument #18) to drastically alleviate current pressures
- The ability to focus our economy & society on shifts in scarcity alleviation suggested above through those technologies
- Current power systems and what is required by everyone on the streets demanding change from the grassroots level

With this understanding we can truly say we have an alternative that is logical, not subject to subjective bias, doesn't rely on the arbitrary game theory of markets and doesn't place some figure on high with absolute power. We can truly say this sample alternative is a true, genuine economical system in that it is designed at its core to focus on equality across the population, ensuring everyone's needs are met, living in dignity. It's core concepts are designed with sustainability inherent, driving our species into equilibrium with the environment, achieving homeostasis with our beautiful planet.

These reforms won't diminish these powerful institutions on their own, we have to demand it, this is the true task of a human rights movement in the 21st century. Nothing is more important a task for our species as we go into what could be a very tumultuous 21st century if nothing is done now, if we don't act now, if we don't adapt now.

In Appendix A I suggest a practical action plan and in Appendix B a practical area of research on this topic. Obviously just rudimentary examples I've conjured, both need lots of work, but the point is the conversation, the collaboration and the cooperation among as many individuals as possible. With individuals that are as full as I am with indignation for the current throes of the power structures that control us and destroy our beautiful planet. Individually we are weak, in solidarity we are strong. They won't hand it over to us, but let's proclaim to them: 'The party is over' (#thepartyisover) and take it from them! See you on the streets.

APPENDIX A- THE GALVANISE-THE-LEFT PROJECT

Organisations Utilising Multi-lateral Think Tanks in Democratic Open Source workspaces to tackle the common problem of ending global oppression and reinventing the economy for true equality and planetary homeostasis

A BRIEF CRITIQUE OF THE UN-GALVANISED LEFT TODAY

We can break this into two parts

1. An unrealistic left
2. A folk politics left

First, to clarify, I consider myself on the 'left'; simply in that I'm full of indignation with any injustice or oppression. I recognise contemporary capitalism as an economic system of oppression, which first and foremost economises oppression in the interest of the few at the expense of the many and the environment. I don't, however, agree that any branch of the various propositions put forward now or in the past could solve global poverty and environmental degradation on it's own. There is no single answer, no silver bullet. All there is; is what works and what doesn't. Only a galvanised left focused on the core issue of ending oppression can make any significant attack on the 'right' (meaning the economics of oppression/enforced global poverty and environmental degradation).

On Point 1:
I don't presume to live in a fantasy world, where some, I feel, on the left do. They seem to pose their version of economics will also (on top of removing the oppression described) achieve a higher standard of efficiency in providing goods and services than capitalism. Capitalism is a function of coercing the vast majority into, essentially, slavery, in the service of the minority. This produces an exceptional level of quality of service for the lucky

ones. It also consumes resources exceptionally quickly which produces a high quantity of goods, again for the lucky ones but at the expense of the environment and devastatingly so.

The critique of capitalism does not purpose we can consume earths resources more efficiently and provide a better service than their slaves can to an opulent few, rather it is just that we endeavour to create a system to be free of that oppression, living in dignity and integrity, but we also recognise we don't need a private jet.

If you're living in the west, it has been calculated that on average a westerner will have between 40-80 slaves working indirectly for them through the supply chain[71], regardless if you're 'woke' or not. The luxuries we in the west enjoy, and these are obviously on a scale where the top 0.1% have the most amount of slavery attached to their lifestyles, are a function of oppression through supply chain slavery. One can minimise the quantity of slaves in their personal supply chain, where they can be at the bottom end of the scale, but just being alive in the developed world submerged in a global financialised market capitalistic world means you privilege from some form of oppression. The left need to accept that and not posit, sometimes arrogantly from a position of privilege, that they can achieve the same quality of service and production of goods as capitalism without any oppression. It basically amounts to hypocrisy and is reductive and false.

What needs to be understood is that a higher standard of living, in terms of the value system that is contemporary today (i.e. owning a yacht) is not what a true high standard of living means in real terms. A higher standard of living means healthy, educated people that through their vocation in life are happy and relatively wealthy with what truly matters; family, friends, health, community. An economic system that removes poverty, protects the environment *and* provides a reasonable level of luxury items and creature

comforts is perfectly feasible, even within the left 'orthodox'
economic systems.

So the argument against contemporary capitalism is that we want to
live in a world of integrity and human dignity, free of oppression,
subjugation and the endless destruction of the environment while
achieving a high standard of living (not in the current paradigms
value system). It is not, also, that we can all have yachts too.

It might seem I'm being facetious here, but I'm just dramatizing to
highlight a major flaw in the lefts argument as I see it, in the interest
of highlighting that orthodox economic systems as a whole are
flawed, at their roots, regardless of what version you advocate.

I *can* imagine an eco-libertarian socialist model achieving a very
high standard of living, with equality and within environmental
limits. However, the core of the economic assumptions still rest on a
Malthusian basis where there isn't enough to go around, the
difference is just sharing it out equally instead of the capitalistic
model of unequal distribution. The focus is not on minimising
scarcity; it is just an output or side effect. I just feel it will eventually
revert back to oppression of some form, compounded by the initial
need to trade within the free market capitalistic system.

We have seen what 'they' do to any nation trying to nationalise and
live socially.
Cuba or Venezuela a case in point. Cuba, however, have achieved a
great standard of living in terms of health and education, trumping
other Latin American countries on some metrics, like infant
mortality rates and literacy, as referenced before, yet they still
struggle due to economic sanctions etc. and are being slowly
eroded; a desperate shame but exemplary of the point in question.

It's my position that only through the application of a genuine
economic system, that is focused on taming scarcity, can we achieve
a situation where we have a maximum standard of living, without
oppression and within environmental limits that are in-depth, will
be enduring and fundamentally doesn't *require* trade with
capitalistic nations (require is highlighted on purpose, any
transition to a better system will have to have a foot on each side of
the door for a time I assume).

The second point is on 'folk-politics':
Folk politics was coined by Nick Srnicek and Alex Williams in their
book *'Inventing the Future: Postcapitalism and a World Without Work'.*
The definition, taken from Wikileaks, which I assume they wrote or
confirmed because the definition seems apt: *'folk politics tends to
privilege reacting to change (through protest and resistance) over
imagining new long-term goals; the immediate and tangible over the
abstract; personal involvement in direct action over institutional
responses; single issues over complex strategies; horizontal organising over
hierarchical; and the local over the large-scale. While arguing that these
approaches are important and can at times be effective, Srnicek and
Williams argue that they are insufficient to tackle global capitalism and
specifically neoliberalism.'*

So, in the interest of not belabouring the point, it's simple really: If
you've just read this for the first time and you consider yourself
'woke', let me politely request you understand that being 'woke'
just is not enough.
It is great to be a vegan, to stop buying first hand sweat shop
clothes, to purchase local grown produce, to take your money out of
international banks and to put it into credit unions or building
societies etc. but the point is we're fighting an international
rampaging beast of devastation that is relentless and ruthless. We
need a fully galvanised, informed, active and engaged left not just a

bunch of individuals trying to out woke each other and secluding themselves to off the grid communes with compost toilets.

Getting on the streets to protest an issue is great but a large-scale strategy where an attempt to control or dismantle the power structure is also necessary, from the inside. It was trade unions who started the labour movement and have won all the working conditions we enjoy today, they understood early on that striking, protesting etc. is not sufficient, the Labour party was born out of that and has been instrumental in all those reforms.

So, to all you well meaning leftists, please don't just join a commune and sell bracelets for your life, don't just buy a small plot of land and live off the grid in a permaculture garden. Do it, but do it while also joining a trade union, being involved in left activism, supporting whatever large scale endeavour you feel is tackling the problem of global oppression on a national &/or international scale. First step; do your research on what that might be.

I feel, which I agree with Srnicek and Williams, a Mont Pelerin society of the left is required. This *Galvanise-the-left project* I've conjured up here is my attempt to join the conversation. So that we may be as well equipped and as strong as possible when this brutal neo-liberal experiment they're currently conducting comes crashing down on their heads. Within that vacuum, we'll be ready.

So then, briefly allow me pose a couple of questions to the left reading this and who are still not convinced:
1.)
If the preconditions and assumptions on scarcity still exist in your proposed economic model, won't it then just be a matter of time and a natural gravitation back to oppression in some form?

My opinion on that would be:

If the assumption is that scarcity is rigid and universal then no matter what model you incorporate after that will require an application of an ideological system to allocate those universally and rigidly scarce resources. If there's always 'not enough to go around' then it's not hard to see a gravitation to an unequal allocation or at least misallocation of life supporting resources, in the sense that the goal would not be to provide an abundance of those resources hence never achieving a true situation of the removal of scarcity and it's resulting poverty.

Each economic model for each nation with their own climate, culture etc. makes it abundantly complex, nuanced and can't be judged without taking in all complex systemic issues on a case-by-case basis. But, in my opinion, even a libertarian socialist model (exampled above as), in the real world (i.e. submerged & required to trade in the dominant economic model of free market capitalism) would return to oppression in some form or another due to myriad pressures on it. A genuine economic model, I believe, would be far more resistant.

Until we have an economic system devote on taming scarcity, creating abundance within resource limits literally embedded in the fundamental equation of the economic model, we will not achieve long-standing results that achieve a status of on-going adaptation and improvement. That, however, is just my opinion and completely up to you to decide of course.

2.)

If trade still exists in the contemporary sense, i.e. markets & money (hence profits) in some form or another, can we really expect there to be a complete removal of coercion and manipulation? Can we really expect the lines of morals and ethics to be respected?

My opinion:

If there is the ability to achieve any sort of advantage, through any scale of competition in a 'market' then we will gravitate again, from a hypothesised socialist nation, back to a situation where peoples 'free will' will be compromised, peoples lines of morals will again be threatened against the threats of 'losing', in whatever way that may look. Ethics will be thwarted to suit the dominant and it will revert to abuse, exploitation and oppression.

Again, I purpose only a genuine economic system, that has no market at all and no money, is the only way to achieve a true situation of freedom, free of coercion and manipulation with long standing core results.

Just to clarify in summary, It is not about right and left, it's about what works:

The right states:

There's not enough to go round, fight for it, some can be wealthy, the weak suffer what they must.

The left states:

There's not enough to go around, let's share it equally, we'll all be o.k, the strong will support the weak.

A genuine economic system; taking a structuralist perspective on socioeconomic management states:

There's plenty to go around with the proper application of technology, for everyone, everyone will have a very high standard of living (in real terms not in current value distortion terms) and that standard will increase as more advanced forms of technology and design/ production/distribution/recycling/ etc. methods become available.

The moral goal of society, and I like to presume even the right agree on this, is to end poverty. The right are happy with an indifferent matter of cause trickle down effect. The left devote their very being to attacking the rights failures yet can't produce, well, haven't produced a working system (regardless of the nuances- Spanish Cataluña 1936 a great example) to end poverty. A genuine economic system simply states the practical and technical way that can be achieved is with the focus of economic activity on that exact goal: removing poverty within environmental limits.

The reason this book seems to attack the right and not the left is because there is no common ground with the right.
Where it is in conjunction with the left is that it is the fight to end that current oppression propagated by the right. If we can galvanise to end oppression while living sustainably then we can have the discussion on the optimum mode of resource allocation at our leisure. So to the left, let us please galvanise and end oppression once and for all? This project I've conjured is my attempt at joining the conversation.

My point in conclusion to the left is this: there may be some branches of the left that feel and I might agree would really incorporate a functioning society free of oppression. Eco-socialism, abundantly described by the late and great Murray Bookchin, is another shining example. But there are *SO* many branches and differences that we can't hope to achieve anything without solidarity on the core issue and in an offense to a now global rampaging right. The right is pretty much in solidarity on their core issue of 'open everything to competition and let the winners win' but the left bickers over nuances or retreats to off-the-grid communes. My point, and apologies for rambling, is that we all have the same goal of ending oppression; this needs to be addressed through the reformation of the precondition or root socioeconomic orientation that produces oppression in a galvanised non-folk politics engaged fashion. With oppression ended and assuming we're living sustainably as a species, we can then bicker over the nuances of assemblies, community structure and how we can maximise democracy.

Recognition, amalgamation and galvanisation of all organisations, individuals and institutions that try to tackle, in their own way, the common problem of global oppression in its many forms. The focus of the galvanisation project however is an effort to tackle the core problem: inequality and its socioeconomic root orientation of 'competition over perceived scarce resources'.

As it's understood, and will be by stakeholders that 'sign-on', that this precondition produces *ALL* the symptoms that we are all currently railing against in our own way.

Competition over perceived scarce resources produces a system of exploitation of human labour through individual profiting- individual profiting through exploitation of labour produces inequality- inequality produces poverty- poverty produces disease, pre-mature death, violence- violence produces bigotry, racism, discrimination and xenophobia amongst others.

Competition over perceived scarce resources produces a system of exploitation through individual profiting- individual profiting produces a societal disregard for externalities- externalities include animals, water, the atmosphere, rivers, soil and rainforests amongst others. In short; resources that sustain human life.

GOALS

Ending global oppression and reinventing the economy for true equality and planetary homeostasis

The recognition that the environmental system is a system of resources, it has limits and functions as a whole structure. No amount of words, songs, poems, fiction, prayers, festivals of love, governmental slogans or community grow hubs will solve the technical problem of a complex networked closed system. The individuals concern for recycling nor corporate goals of carbon offsetting nor the UNs Sustainable development goals will solve the core technical resource production & distribution problems we currently suffer.

Only a technical solution with an understanding of the environment system as a whole and it's myriad functions, rules, caveats, limits and parameters will suffice. We are all just nodes in that overall system, currently operating on an individualistic level. How we operate as a group needs to be programmed, we need an algorithm that meets the rules and parameters of the system within which we sit.

An economic system is merely a word we have invented to describe our interaction with the environmental system.
If the environment, and our technology, produces X amount of resources, our equation on how we operate within that limit as a group needs to remain within that limit. So first a calculation of what X is, is prudent and the first step. Our interaction with X must then consider how we produce, process, distribute, consume and recycle said resource using the Best Available Technology Not Exceeding Environmental Limits (BATNEEL) we currently have at our disposable.

The resulting level of resource X is it's true level of scarcity at that given moment. Hence we arrive at high school level algebra: Resource X on the left of the equals and an equation taking all those requirements stated above on the right. This is a true or *genuine economic* system, in the truest sense of the word. Nothing is up for debate in that. In the same sense that nothing is up for debate when you say the square root of 25 is 5.

This concept is detailed in abundantly more detail in Chapter 5 and Appendix B of the book by Peter Joseph; *'The New Human Rights Movement'*.

METHOD

When signing in, the stakeholder agrees to help tackle the core problem and agrees to vote upon solutions & improvements to each workspace of transition posed. At minimum agree at first to apportion 10% of their resources to the core problem, rather than to symptoms, and gradually increase along specific increments pre-agreed practically.
#galvanisetheleft

THINK TANK STRUCTURE EXAMPLE:

- Open source workspaces to create, edit and amalgamate work multi-laterally
- Stakeholders involved will 'sign into' topics of interest
- Voting on most advanced response to questions or most apt solution to problems posed in the respective think tank
- Improvements to the answer/solution then voted upon to be accepted,
- Organisations involved are obliged to vote in assistance of their peers (email sent when improvement made).
- Overtime the best, democratically approved and accepted approach is produced by everyone
- Involved groups can then work together in achieving approved targets/goals/objectives (10% resource etc.)

1. **Transitioning to automation**
   a. From Labour for income emphasis to machine automation emphasis
2. **Transitioning to an access economy**
   a. From private property/ownership to access of resources
   b. Maximize good-use time efficiency
   c. Reduce production pressure (resource consumption reduction)
3. **Transitioning cities & communities**
   a. Globalisation to Localisation (networked design)
   b. Max production/distribution efficiency
4. **Transitioning work places**
   a. From Patents, IPs and information hoarding to Open source collaborative commons
   b. Participatory democratic economics
5. **Transitioning resource production**
   a. From fragmented economic feedback to networked digital, fully integrated, sensor based feedback economics.
      i. Using the optimum in Algorithmic calculations
6. **Tackling the neo-liberal dogma**
   a. Understanding the biopyschosocial human condition and using that knowledge to inspire social activism & economic change
   b. Using current public institutions to devolve 'too big to fail' private powers to equilibrium, then devolve both and spread the power equitably
   c. Creating a 'Mont Pelerine Society' of the left

From Labour-for-income emphasis to Machine Automation emphasis. In the current system we would need to incorporate a Universal basic Access economy funded through the funding approach described in the Universal basic dividend idea to keep people fed & watered while machines/robots do rudimentary works, taking jobs. DEY TURK ER JUUURBS! Jobs are not what people need, what jobs give people is what's required. i.e. A LIFE

- Maximise productive capacity in a sustainable fashion
    - Hence minimising poverty (in a real sense)
- Reduce human exposure
    - The less attractive, monotonous or arduous the labour is the more machine automation will be focused on it, on an ever-increasing scale/rate.
- Increase efficiency
    - Doing more and more with less and less ('ephemeralisation' as coined by Buck Minster Fuller some 70 years ago).

Follow me on this thought process to the end before you make an opinion please:

A.) Leave your current values and preconceptions (brainwashed since birth in capitalism) at the door, use your imagination to extrapolate for society:

There's currently $81trillion dollars in global GDP, and 8 people have the same monetary wealth as 50% of the global population. If we were to evenly distribute that wealth, even in the current system of incentivised domination, one can imagine a lifestyle akin to a middle class family in the west for everyone.

Of course this is outrageously opposite to the current systems mechanics of domination and inequality, sacrosanct. Further, if everyone lived in the current system as middle class westerners live we would need 27 Earths by 2050 to provide that quantity of resources, as stated before.

The fact remains, we COULD live without poverty. So the question is then: how is the system structured, creating poverty? The answer is exploitation and waste. With the full use of technology in a system of equitable distribution of basic resources, focusing on these 5 key points you can provide a *'middle class'* standard of living for everyone while remaining in the planets limits.

Obviously, a change in values will need to be recognised, where the 'dissatisfaction' is recognised and that you do not need a yacht, two Ferraris and a private jet. But everyone does have food, clean water, shelter and energy. That can be achieved very soon. A sensible middle class standard of living can be achieved.

Use machines, computers and robots to their full potential. *They don't take your jobs away they alleviate arduous labour.*
The problem is access to resources, that is a socio-economic problem not a technological problem.

THEME 2- ACCESS

From Property ownership emphasis to strategic access emphasis

- Maximise good (e.g. a car) use-time efficiency

- Minimises production pressure
  - Hence minimising resource consumption and waste
- Increase over-all good availability for use

Follow this thought process of logic here please:

Say we have a city of 100,000 people. 10,000 of them play tennis. 9,000 play the odd time. 900 play once a week. 90 play 2-3 times a week. And 10 are professionals. Let's say we've done the calculations and found that 100 tennis courts is sufficient to always have a place for them to play at anytime they want. How many tennis rackets do we need to manufacture?
If you said 10,000 please go back to A.

Yes, the correct answer is 400. Maybe we can argue for an extra 10% for good measure. So 440. 4 rackets needed per court to play doubles if desired.

Let's say a standard racket requires:
- 10 grams of nylon
- 1 kg of aluminium
- 10 grams of rubber
- 1 gram of tungsten

The BATNEEL model requires:
- 10 grams of nylon
- 1 kg of aluminium
- 10 grams of rubber
- 5 grams of tungsten

Therefore we can now say we need to make 90% of the 440 in standard models because the people who play the odd time won't mind having a racket that has zero impact to resources (would be calculated obviously for each good). And so on respectively until the avid players request and use the BAT model.

When the system accounts for the full quantity of resources available (caveat hurdle: we would need *to proclaim earths resources as common heritage*). Then uses that information to provide models of goods that are BAT but not exceeding environmental limits (BATNEEL) then we have true good availability. A true level of scarcity.

But I would argue that we would have a true level of 'abundance' if you can follow me again for a simple thought process:
In the current system of private property, think of the 9,000 tennis rackets currently sitting in the corner of some garage doing nothing for 99% of their lives, the others that even though used by a pro still probably are only in use 25% of the time. Think of the quantity of nylon, rubber, aluminium, tungsten, human labour and GHGs used to create it all. Now, think of ALL the goods in the world sitting around doing nothing. The millions of cars parked up doing nothing. Pure waste.

In a system strategically-sustainable, emphasising access over ownership, huge resource consumption decreases will be seen. So, that part of your brain that I know said: 'everyone will want the 'BATNEEL' (if you're still convinced of this go back to A) becomes invalid, as the resources saved from the current system will produce an exceptional 'standard model'. Compounded by the quantity if resources saved by not producing the 8,560 rackets.

Further, if you compound this by letting the 10,000 tennis enthusiasts have a say in what tennis racket they would like to play with, in an open source fashion, you will constantly see a level of satisfaction and improvement on the quality of the standard model, that will surely trump anything you see today in no time.

Would you agree with the following statement in this regard then: *True technological progress within the planets limits. True sustainability.*

THEME 3- OPEN SOURCE

From data hoarding, proprietary research, internal development (patents and Intellectual Property (IP) rights) to collaborative commons
  - Maximise innovation

Cooperation through the group mind has been proven to solve problems more efficiently[72] than competition or the individual expert. Nothing could be more innately logical to me; surprised this even needs to be said.

Thought process:
Imagine every car manufacturer sharing info on the latest advancements in technology that they have researched. Further, imagine a system where sustainability is a pre-requisite to manufacture. One can envision extremely efficient cars, high performance, with universal parts that can be easily fixed (imagine an engine that can be easily removed and fixed with standard processes and parts across the industry).

Further, imagine an online system where anyone can go on (me not being one of them but I know 100's of people that would love it as a hobby and more who would do it as a profession if they didn't have the burden of debt looming) and see schematics of the cars, details on latest technologies, parts, resource availability (*proclaiming earths resources as common heritage needed*) and discuss the best models and styles they like. Imagine the car that would be produced. Genuinely top of the range, most liked models, made within the planets limits with universal parts easily changeable and recyclable. The next generation Computer Aided Design (CAD) tool called Dreamcatcher is exemplary of how is this could be done on a large scale with the assistance of computers to come to a conclusion through millions of variables to produce the best outcome within our set parameters of resources etc. Computers are now at a scale to greatly augment our existence, let's stop holding them back with IPs and patents.

Concurrently: the item that some company makes e.g. apple and the iPhone. They don't *own* the intellectual property for this. The people that 'invented' that exact first 'iPhone' weren't just born with all the knowledge of humanity that gave them the base knowledge to manufacture it. In reality, a small part of it 'belongs' to the Egyptians, the Greeks, the Romans, Nostradamus, Da Vinci, James Watt, Alan Turing etc. and those people owe their inventions and brilliance to the people before them. Patents and I.P rights are pure nonsense.

Society owes to society; nothing is in isolation. The surplus of capital is owed to everyone. As goods availability and quality grows so to should the standard of living for all in tandem. One person taking the profit for the combined work of humanity through history and through the current infrastructure (i.e. the schools that taught them and the hospitals that kept them healthy) is plainly just offensive and a disgrace or a mockery to humanity. A pragmatic idea to incorporate this into society is the Universal Basic Access idea funded through the Universal Basic Dividend[73], this will also work perfectly as a solution to technological unemployment as described before in this text.

From globalisation to localisation, emphasising a networked design
- Maximise production/distribution efficiency
  - Huge reduction in waste

Currently it's estimated that about 33% of food produced in the west goes to waste, never makes it to a human stomach. While comparatively about 33% of humanity live in abject poverty, literally starving. So, immediately, this argument of 'hunger is due to nature's inability to provide' is complete nonsense.

There is plenty of food and there is ample technology to provide it. There are working examples of societal structures to organise this, so why are they hungry? Must be just nature. Conversation over.

Poverty has nothing to do with the quantity of bread and everything to do with where that bread is produced and who it is distributed to. Third world countries are exploited for first world benefits. Our decadence is in direct correlation to their degradation. The poor on the streets of Dublin don't have a house due to a lack of housing; they don't have a house because resources or 'houses' are distributed in a certain fashion. i.e. through a historically heinous rigged system of resource distribution from the bottom upwards at an ever-increasing share the further you rise up the hierarchy.

If you said something like 'people are poor because they're lazy and can't budget' please go back to A. better yet, go talk to a homeless person and ask him how he ended up there, with a small bit of intuition one can see a pattern.

Follow this thought process on food production/distribution please: First, if you're reading this and are not a vegetarian/vegan, cop on!

Imagine communities of 150 people max. The OAPs and kids after school run vegetable growing hubs, using all available space including roofs to grow vegetables. If there is not enough space to feed the full community: use vertical farming, aquaponics and all the rest of the immensely beneficial technology we have today. Imagine composting toilets for full circle. The community chips in for solar panels or geothermal and becomes self-sufficient.

A community run kitchen, where everyone's food is cooked in one go. Minimal waste, minimal heating elements, an order of magnitude less GHGs (from transportation especially, I've eaten bananas from Ecuador, no one call tell me technology can't grow bananas down the road form me here in London) and arguably the best bit: community interaction across all ages, instead of lonely individuals.

If this were incorporated by the majority, with a vegetarian diet, we could solve the climate problem overnight.
Obviously this is hugely against the current economic structure of exploiting poor nations for their labour to max profits but again dignity, integrity and respect is the path I wish to choose, do you?

Granted, complexities regarding more complicated luxury goods are apparent but the fact remains that feeding, watering, housing and providing electricity can be achieved locally and easily. The basic necessities of life could easily be provided for everyone, very soon. This should not be a privilege in the 21st century, where as a species we are discussing the behaviour of quarks and supernovae. Technology is obviously at a level to provide a good standard of living for everyone; once this is achieved one can deliberate at leisure on the nuisances of how to have snorkel equipment accessible for the Jones's & the Smith's on Saturday afternoon.

But there is something in technologies way. We all know what it is so let's simply change it. Not *easily* done but it is *simply* done.

Simply: Quantify, produce and distribute earth's resources in a structured, organised, sustainable, localised and equitable fashion.

I know you've just asked it in your head right? When we have reached a level of food security, how do we know how many snorkels to produce…

THEME 5- NETWORKED DIGITAL FEEDBACK

From a fragmented economic data relay to fully integrated sensor-based feedback system
- Maximises feedback and information efficacy/utilisation
  - This will increase total economic efficiency

Currently, the socio-economic system sees resources as an endless pit. There is no part of free market capitalism that questions or polices the recuperation rate of the planets resources. Infinite growth through the consumption of resources is the only goal; maximise individual profit. All negative effects to the planet are in isolation and are externalities.

Each actor in the economic sphere merely acquires products related to demand of desired purchase and try's to sell accordingly for individual gain. This failure of any approach of sustainability is compounded by the competitive nature and the wasteful practices touched upon previously.

Essentially, these isolated economic data tell us nothing about how, where, when and in what quantities resources can be used to maintain sustainability on a finite planet. At its very core our economic system is cancerous, viral.

The most wasteful and idiotic function of our current socio-economic system must be the phenomenon of planned obsolescence. Where companies, acting in complete isolation from one another and with a complete disregard for resource depletion, will purposefully make their product fail so as to ensure a repurchase or a necessity to buy their parts to fix it. Think of the tennis racket analogy above and the quantities of the tungsten etc. wasted, now double that every year as the company requires another instrument of exchange to keep profitable, it designs the product to fail (after the warranty period of course).

In a system of planned feedback, the decision on what is needed to be produced in a holistic fashion would immediately cut out this ridiculous practice. The internet of things discussed in argument #9 would basically put the counterargument mute.
This idea can be used on a global scale with life support resources to give feedback in real-time on what is required when and how. Again, as has been discussed, greatly reducing resource consumption, waste, energy consumption amongst many other benefits over and above the ability of price.

APPENDIX B- SOCIAL MOVEMENT AS A

SOCIAL SCIENCE

Understanding the biopsychosocial human condition to affect the group mind, ensuring constant adaptation to the prerequisites of an ever-changing environment

GOAL

How can we inspire change in the masses through an understanding of the human condition? Can we find the correlation between the mass-mind, group-mind and what drives the group to excel or progress. Can we then tap into whatever that is, nurture, encourage and utilise it to its optimum benefit.

Goal: Attaining homeostasis with the planet by coupling the economic system with the environmental system.

SCOPE

Noting that the biological, physical and social nature of humanity is fully dependant on the environment. Therefore how can we gain an understanding of the human condition and bring the group mind to par with what it depends on?

Currently the biopsychosocial nature of humanity is seen in their sum parts as isolated and in turn each part isolated from the environment with which they rest. Therefore, the proposition is that a social science branch in and of itself dedicated to the understanding of how the group must behave itself on the system with which it interacts with on all of its levels: biological, physical and social <u>and</u> all together. This understanding is required to ensure continued existence on a planet on which life evolved through the 'survival of the fittest' strategic precondition, adaptation to the prerequisites of the environment.

Essentially, Controlling the singular selfish gene in the interest of the larger system, in this case the planet and our longevity on it, is the logical next step in the human condition.

So, we have 2 core components of this study:

Humanity and the planet:

An understanding of the current group mind (society), the current environment (planet carrying capacity) and an understanding of how they currently interact (economic system). From there the study is then on how the group *should* be interacting with the environment. Ergo, what is required to interact correctly?

The main focus of study is then the connection between the 2.

- Current mode of interaction (economy)
- Limits to consumption of resources
  - Regional
  - Global
- Required mode based on limits

The study of 'Humanity' involves the study of:

- The biopsychosocial human condition
  - Human biology
    - Individual
    - group
  - Human psychology
    - Individual
    - Group
  - Human society
    - Past social movements- all revolutions.
      - Common themes
      - Compare and contrast
    - Current social movements
      - Common themes
      - Compare and contrast
  - The connection of all three

- How the group psychology works relating to the other 2

The study of the environment involves the study of:

- Evolution
- Resources
    - Limits
        - Local
        - Regional
        - Global
    - Carrying capacity (current technological application)
        - Local
        - Regional
        - Global
    - Carrying capacity (BATNEEL* application)

Best Available Technology Not Exceeding Environmental Limits

- Then the study must analyse and come up with improvements. Then pose methods of adaptation from the current human-environment interaction (economic system) to an interaction that is in homeostasis.

- This interaction in homeostasis with our planetary system would essentially be a true economic system as described in Appendix A under the heading 'Goals'.

-    Finally from there, and the most difficult, integration in the methodology for this homeostasis interaction to have the ability to adapt any parts or all parts to any changes in the environmental system at any given time.

-    If achieved would be the true meaning of being a 'Fit' species on our beautiful planet.

ENDNOTES

[1] https://www.theguardian.com/books/2016/apr/15/neoliberalism-ideology-problem-george-monbiot

[2] http://www.econport.org/econport/request?page=man_gametheory_exp_prisondil

[3] Joseph, Peter (2017). The new human rights movement. Benbella. 2017, pp 85-8

[4] Sapolsky, Robert, (1998), Why Zebras Don't Get Ulcers, W.H. Freeman., 2017, pp 383

[5] https://www.thenonprofittimes.com/npt_articles/volunteer-time-value-hits-all-time-high/

[6] Robert W. Sussman, C. Robert Cloninger (2011), Origins of Altruism and Cooperation, Springer-Verlag New York

[7] https://www.un.org/en/sections/issues-depth/poverty/

[8] https://www.researchgate.net/publication/44836310_The_Ethical_Poverty_Line_A_Moral_Quantification_of_Absolute_Poverty

[9] https://blogs.worldbank.org/opendata/september-2020-global-poverty-update-world-bank-new-annual-poverty-estimates-using-revised

[10] https://www.theguardian.com/global-development/2017/jan/16/worlds-eight-richest-people-have-same-wealth-as-poorest-50

[11] https://www.trustforlondon.org.uk/data/life-expectancy-borough/

[12] Wilkinson, Richard; Pickett, Kate (2010).**The Spirit Level**: Why Equality is Better for Everyone. Penguin.

[13] https://borgenproject.org/how-much-does-it-cost-to-end-poverty/

[14] Gilbert, Richard, Murphy, Nora A., Stepka, Allison, Barrett, Mark and Worku, Dianne. "Would a Basic Income Guarantee Reduce the Motivation to Work? An Analysis of Labor Responses in 16 Trial Programs" *Basic Income Studies*, vol. 13, no. 2, 2018. https://doi.org/10.1515/bis-2018-0011

[15] https://www.statista.com/statistics/279757/apparel-market-size-projections-by-region/

[16] Bo Ekman, Johan Rockström, and Anders Wijkman, Grasping the Climate Crisis (Stockholm: The Tällberg Foundation, 2008), 8, http://www.tallbergfoundation.org.

[17] Wilkinson, Richard; Pickett, Kate (2010).**The Spirit Level**: Why Equality is Better for Everyone. Penguin., 2010, pp. 284–5

[18] 1900–1940: John W. Kendrick, *Productivity Trends in the United States*. Princeton: Princeton University Press (for NBER), 1961.

[19] https://www.newscientist.com/article/mg21929310-200-state-of-innovation-busting-the-private-sector-myth/

[20] https://www.endwaterpoverty.org/blog/why-can-people-get-access-mobile-phones-and-not-safe-water

[21] http://www.fao.org/3/x0262e/x0262e05.htm

[22] https://news.un.org/en/story/2014/02/461372-illicit-financial-outflows-africa-crippling-continents-development-un

[23] https://www.researchgate.net/publication/44836310_The_Ethical_Poverty_Line_A_Moral_Quantification_of_Absolute_Poverty

24 https://www.epi.org/productivity-pay-gap/

25 Rifkin, J. (2014) The **Zero Marginal Cost Society**. The Internet of Things, the

Collaborative Commons and the Eclipse of Capitalism. New York. Palgrave

26 Kanefsky, B., N.G. Barlow, and V.C. Gulick. (2001). "Can Distributed Volunteers Accomplish Massive Data Analysis Tasks?" *Proceedings of the Lunar and Planetary Science Conference* XXXII

27 https://en.wikipedia.org/wiki/Collective_intelligence#Evidence

28https://www.cbd.int/doc/c/3824/7957/5bb56cbf504e73b6f00282e9/cop-14-1-02-en.pdf

29 https://www.cbd.int/gbo5

30 Mora, Camilo. Sale, Peter F. Vol. 434 (July 28 2011), Ongoing global biodiversity loss and the need to move beyond protected areas: Marine Ecology Progress Series pp. 251-266 (16 pages), Inter-Research Science Center

31 https://corporateeurope.org/en/international-trade/2019/01/take-action-strike-blow-against-corporate-power-2019

32 Hobsbawn, Eric. 2011, How to change the world,. Littlebrown, 2011, pp 11

33 "Chile: Anatomy of an economic miracle, 1970-1986". *libcom.org*. Retrieved Sep 14, 2020

34 Butkiewicz, James. Yanikkaya, Halit (2005) *The Effects of IMF and*

World Bank Lending on Long-Run Economic Growth: An Empirical Analysis. World Development 33(3):371-391

[35] https://www.marketplace.org/2021/01/19/why-rich-people-tend-think-they-deserve-their-money/

[36] Sachs, Jeffery (2006). The End of Poverty: Economic Possibilities for Our Time. Penguin.

[37] http://naturalcapitalcoalition.org/wp-content/uploads/2016/07/Trucost-Nat-Cap-at-Risk-Final-Report-web.pdf

[38] https://www.forbes.com/billionaires/

[39] https://www.thelondoneconomic.com/news/environment/poor-people-really-are-more-charitable-than-the-rich-according-to-new-research-93441/

[40] https://www.vox.com/future-perfect/2019/9/3/20840955/charitable-deduction-tax-rich-billionaire-philanthropy

[41] https://www.visualcapitalist.com/debt-to-gdp-continues-to-rise-around-world/

[42]*Perkins, John, 1945-. (2004). Confessions of an economic hit man.* San Francisco, CA :Berrett-Koehler.

[43] Klien, Naomi. (2007). The **shock doctrine**: The rise of **disaster capitalism**. Toronto: Alfred A. Knopf Canada

[44] Adorno, T. and Horkheimer, M., (1944). Frankfurt School: The Culture Industry: Enlightenment as Mass Deception. [online] Available at:
https://www.marxists.org/reference/archive/adorno/1944/culture-

industry.htm

[45] https://www.theguardian.com/global-development-professionals-network/2017/jan/14/aid-in-reverse-how-poor-countries-develop-rich-countries

[46] Posani, Balamuralidhar. (2009). *Crisis in the Countryside: Farmer Suicides and The Political Economy of Agrarian Distress in India.* [online] available at: www.lse.ac.uk/depts/destin

[47] *Perkins, John, 1945-. (2004). Confessions of an economic hit man.* San Francisco, CA :Berrett-Koehler.

[48] https://news.un.org/en/story/2014/02/461372-illicit-financial-outflows-africa-crippling-continents-development-un

[49] Herman, E. S., & Chomsky, N. (1988). *Manufacturing consent: The political economy of the mass media.* New York: Pantheon Books.

[50] https://eh.net/encyclopedia/the-economic-impact-of-the-black-death/

[51] Brierley, Geraldene Louise. (2017). Subconscious Marketing Techniques: the implications for consumer regulations and the marketing profession. [online] available at: https://repository.cardiffmet.ac.uk/bitstream/handle/10369/8781/FINAL%20Thesis%20Submission_Brierley%20%28002%29.pdf?sequence=1&isAllowed=y

[52] https://www.project-syndicate.org/commentary/basic-income-funded-by-capital-income-by-yanis-varoufakis-2016-10?barrier=accessreg

[53] Anna Coote (2021) Universal basic services and sustainable

consumption, Sustainability: Science, Practice and Policy, 17:1, 32-46, DOI: 10.1080/15487733.2020.1843854

[54] https://www.wsj.com/articles/SB10001424052702303763804579183680751473884

[55] Jones, Adam. (2019). Genocide and Structural Violence: Charting the Terrain

[56] Kohler, G., & Alcock, N. (1976). An Empirical Table of Structural Violence. Journal of Peace Research, 13(4), 343–356. https://doi.org/10.1177/002234337601300405

[57] http://www.amazon.com/Violence-Reflections-Our-Deadliest-Epidemic/dp/1849850658

[58] https://blackrosefed.org/spain-anarchism-in-action/

[59] https://www.who.int/countries/cub/

[60] https://www.coha.org/hugo-chavez-and-the-future-of-venezuela/

[61] Wilkinson, Richard; Pickett, Kate (2010). The Spirit Level: Why Equality is Better for Everyone. Penguin.

[62] Wilkinson, Richard; Pickett, Kate. (2018) The Inner Level: How More Equal Societies Reduce Stress, Restore Sanity and Improve Everyone's Well-Being. Penguin,

[63] https://www.youtube.com/watch?v=Qf92l7FPyKo

[64] Maté, Gabor (2003). *When the body says no, exploring the stress disease connection*. Wiley.

[65] Wackernagel, Mathis, et al. "Tracking the ecological overshoot of the human economy." Proceedings of the national Academy of Sciences 99.14 (2002): 9266-9271.

66 https://www.oecd.org/env/indicators-modelling-outlooks/oecdenvironmentaloutlookto2050theconsequencesofinaction-keyfactsandfigures.htm

67 https://www.bccresearch.com/market-research/pharmaceuticals/global-cancer-therapeutics-market-emphasis-on-recurrent-and-metastatic-divisions.html

68 https://www.britannica.com/biography/Norman-Borlaug

69 www.thevenusproject.com

70 www.bfi.org

71 https://www.antislavery.org/slavery-today/slavery-in-global-supply-chains/

72 https://en.wikipedia.org/wiki/Collective_intelligence#Evidence

73 https://www.project-syndicate.org/commentary/basic-income-funded-by-capital-income-by-yanis-varoufakis-2016-10?barrier=accessreg